SUCCESS *Savvy*

ADRIANA LUNA CARLOS
Editor-In-Chief, Designer
and Co-Founder

HANNA OLIVAS
Managing Editor &
Co-Founder

NICOLE CURTIS
Director of the SRS
Magazine Division

ADVERTISING OPPORTUNITIES
Info@SheRisesStudios.com

SUCCESS SAVVY MAGAZINE
APRIL 2025

SHE RISES
STUDIOS

CONTACT US
SheRisesStudios@gmail.com

WWW.SHERISESSTUDIOS.COM

LETTER FROM THE EDITORS

Dear Reader,

Welcome to the April 2025 edition of Success Savvy Magazine, where we're diving deep into the theme: *Financial Futures: Empowering Path to Wealth and Success*. In this issue, we're exploring what it truly means to achieve financial independence—not just in terms of wealth, but in the freedom and confidence it brings.

We're thrilled to feature KB Vega on this month's cover. Her journey—from NYC nightlife to building InspiHER Empire, a thriving fashion and lifestyle brand—is a powerful testament to resilience, bold entrepreneurship, and unwavering self-belief. KB's story embodies the spirit of this edition: turning passion into profit and purpose into power.

Throughout these pages, you'll find inspiring stories from entrepreneurs, thought leaders, and innovators who are redefining success. Whether you're scaling your startup, seeking smarter investments, or simply striving for a more fulfilling financial future, this issue offers practical tips and fresh ideas to help you thrive.

At Success Savvy, we believe financial independence is more than numbers—it's about creating a life of meaning, freedom, and impact. Let this edition inspire you to chase your boldest ambitions and build a future that reflects your true potential.

Warm regards,

Adriana Luna Carlos and Hanna Olivas
Editors of Success Savvy Magazine

SHE RISES STUDIOS

FENIX TV

she wins
NICE GIRLS FINISH FIRST

SHE WINS
VIRTUAL SUMMIT 2025

When: May 14–16, 2025
Where: Exclusively on FENIX TV
Tickets: $49.97

Join us for the **She Wins Virtual Summit 2025**, a 3-day event celebrating women entrepreneurs and leaders from around the world. This year's theme, **"Nice Girls Finish First,"** showcases how kindness, empathy, and integrity drive success in business and life.

What to Expect:

- Inspiring stories from women leaders.
- Expert advice on leadership, resilience, and growth.
- Strategies for thriving in business without compromising values.

BE PART OF THIS EMPOWERING MOVEMENT AND DISCOVER HOW KINDNESS LEADS TO GREATNESS!

WWW.SHERISESSTUDIOS.COM/SHEWINSVIRTUALSUMMIT2025

FROM HUSTLE TO PURPOSE:

THE WOMAN BEHIND INSPIHER EMPIRE

In the heart of Boston, a movement is reshaping the way women embrace confidence, self-love, and empowerment. At the forefront is KB Vega, the founder of InspiHER Empire, a brand that has grown beyond fashion into a symbol of resilience and authenticity. Her journey, however, was anything but conventional.

For five years, KB Vega thrived in New York City's nightlife industry. However, beneath the surface, she battled personal challenges that left her feeling lost. She eventually moved back to Boston to support her then-boyfriend, now husband, Anthony, as he pursued his dream of opening a restaurant. While he built his vision, she sought stability in a nine-to-five job, landing a role at the hospital where she was born. However, the corporate environment left her unfulfilled, and she longed for something more meaningful.

In 2018, KB Vega made the bold decision to leave her job and start a positivity platform on Instagram. She shared her struggles with addiction, trauma, loss, and abuse, never expecting the overwhelming response she received. Women reached out, expressing gratitude for her vulnerability. This support made her realize her true calling—empowering women to embrace their self-worth.

Combining this mission with her passion for fashion, she launched InspiHER Empire, a clothing brand promoting self-love, body positivity, and confidence. More than just apparel, her brand became a movement, encouraging women to feel beautiful and empowered.

Growing up in a large Italian family where food was central, KB Vega struggled with body image from a young age. This led to self-esteem issues, eating disorders, and addiction. For years, she sought validation in unhealthy ways, feeling as if she was never enough. The pain she endured now fuels her mission—to ensure that no woman suffers in silence trying to feel *"good enough."* InspiHER Empire is not just about fashion; it's about creating a space where women feel supported at every stage of their journey.

Balancing entrepreneurship while helping run a restaurant with her husband was challenging. Since InspiHER Empire was self-funded, she relied on restaurant income to sustain her business. However, working long hours in the restaurant left little time for her growing brand.

When the restaurant closed in November 2024 due to an unstable lease agreement, it was a devastating blow. Their primary income source disappeared overnight, forcing them to reassess their future. Yet, in hindsight, the closure became a blessing. KB Vega could finally dedicate herself fully to InspiHER Empire, and despite the challenges, she and her husband found themselves in a healthier, more balanced place.

KB Vega's journey to self-acceptance was not easy. She reached a breaking point where she realized that no one was coming to save her—she had to take control of her own destiny. Hitting rock bottom forced her to make changes. The process was long and painful, but she chose herself every day, even when it felt impossible.

Her advice to other women is simple: stop waiting for the perfect moment; just start. Healing is messy, uncomfortable, and difficult, but it is always worth it. Setting boundaries, surrounding oneself with positive people, and recognizing self-worth are crucial steps to self-love.

InspiHER Empire is more than a clothing brand—it is a movement focused on confidence and boldness. Living fearlessly means embracing authenticity and refusing to shrink for others' comfort.

KB Vega encourages women to stop second-guessing themselves, take risks, and trust their power. Confidence is not about perfection—it's about moving forward despite insecurities. Her brand's designs reflect this mindset, helping women feel strong, capable, and unstoppable.

Fashion has always been a tool for KB Vega. In the past, she used clothing to hide her insecurities, but now, she uses it to uplift others. InspiHER Empire is designed to help women feel seen and fearless. When they wear her designs, she wants them to feel unstoppable. For her, the brand is not about selling apparel—it's about instilling the mindset that says, *"I am powerful, and I refuse to play small."*

Building a community around self-love has been transformative, not just for her customers but for herself. What began as a mission to help others also contributed to her own healing. The women who connect with her message inspire her every day, reinforcing the importance of her work. InspiHER Empire has become more than just a brand—it's a sisterhood where women uplift one another.

Beyond entrepreneurship, KB Vega and her husband document their travels through Trippin' It With the KB Vegas. Travel has been essential in their relationship, allowing them to reconnect and escape the daily grind. When they owned the restaurant, their time together was limited, making their trips even more meaningful. These adventures strengthened their bond and shaped KB Vega's perspective on life and business. She believes that while hard work is necessary, truly living is just as important. Her passion for travel aligns with InspiHER Empire's mission—to encourage women to embrace confidence, adventure, and a fearless approach to life.

Through her journey, KB Vega has learned that self-doubt is often the biggest obstacle to success. Initially, she thought the hardest parts of business would be marketing or sales, but she quickly realized that overcoming her own fears was the real challenge. Trusting the process and pushing forward despite setbacks became the key to her growth. Her advice to aspiring entrepreneurs is to start before they feel ready. Waiting for perfection leads to stagnation. She encourages women to take action, stay consistent, and, most importantly, believe in themselves.

Looking ahead, KB Vega envisions InspiHER Empire becoming a global movement. She hopes to expand the brand, create spaces for women to connect, and host events that foster empowerment and support. Her mission remains the same: to remind women of their power and worth. The journey has not been easy, but her unwavering belief in her purpose keeps her moving forward. InspiHER Empire is not just about fashion—it's about changing lives, one confident woman at a time.

CONNECT WITH KB VEGA

www.instagram.com/inspiherempire
www.facebook.com/inspiherempire
www.inspiherempire.com
kbvega@inspiherempire.com

IG for Trippin' It With The Vegas is:
@trippinitwiththevegas
www.facebook.com/trippinitwiththevegas

WINE OF THE TIMES:

AI NOW PREDICTS YOUR PERFECT POUR

BY MERILEE KERN

ABOUT THE AUTHOR:

Merilee Kern, MBA is an internationally-regarded brand strategist and analyst who reports on noteworthy industry change makers, movers, shakers and innovators across all B2B and B2C categories. This includes field experts and thought leaders, brands, products, services, destinations and events. Merilee is Founder, Executive Editor and Producer of *"The Luxe List."* As a prolific business and consumer trends, lifestyle and leisure industry voice of authority and tastemaker, she keeps her finger on the pulse of the marketplace in search of new and innovative must-haves and exemplary experiences at all price points, from the affordable to the extreme—also delving into the minds behind the brands. Her work reaches multi-millions worldwide via broadcast TV (her own shows and copious others on which she appears) as well as a myriad of print and online publications. Some or all of the accommodations(s), experience(s), item(s) and/or service(s) detailed above may have been provided or arranged at no cost to accommodate if this is review editorial, but all opinions expressed are entirely those of Merilee Kern and have not been influenced in any way.

Imagine having a seasoned sommelier at your fingertips—one who understands your personal taste, predicts your preferences, and guides you to the perfect bottle of wine every time. This is no longer a fantasy. BetterAI, the Silicon Valley disruptor in artificial intelligence, has launched VinoVoss, an AI-powered sommelier that is not just shaking up the wine industry, but redefining how we discover and enjoy wine.

VinoVoss—available as an app and on the web—represents a paradigm shift in wine selection, leveraging cutting-edge AI and natural language processing to deliver highly personalized wine recommendations. From novices to connoisseurs, users can now easily navigate the vast world of wine with a virtual sommelier that adapts to their unique tastes. Whether you're looking for the perfect pairing for a romantic dinner or simply exploring new varietals, VinoVoss delivers recommendations that feel tailor-made.

This innovation couldn't come at a better time. As the U.S. wine market is projected to reach $39 billion in 2024, VinoVoss is poised to capitalize on the growing trend of wine as an everyday indulgence, rather than just a luxury for special occasions. By simplifying the wine selection process, VinoVoss is making wine more accessible and enjoyable for everyone, from the curious beginner to the seasoned expert.

But VinoVoss isn't just about convenience—it's about enhancing the wine experience. The tool picks the perfect wine for any occasion courtesy of a highly advanced artificial intelligence architecture. It leverages advanced artificial intelligence to act as your personal sommelier, providing tailored wine recommendations based on your unique taste preferences, occasion, and budget.

VinoVoss understands that the process of selecting wine can be overwhelming. The breadth of viniculture is challenging to navigate without a skilled guide, and the subjective nature of taste has long stumped traditional search engines. The VinoVoss platform provides a solution, combining the power of AI with the knowledge of sommeliers in a pocket-size package. The app's signature feature, Smart Somm, is an AI-powered chatbot trained by world-renowned sommeliers, ready to answer any wine-related questions and guide you to the perfect bottle. The interactive Smart Somm chat intelligently assists in wine exploration, answers questions, and provides educational insight. The database is continually updated and monitored by the VinoVoss team of wine experts and sommeliers to keep up-to-date with today's wine trends. From beginner to seasoned devotee, this search engine is a powerful and streamlined tool to help users build knowledge and shop, sip, and savor.

With an intuitive interface, VinoVoss allows users to search for wines by grape variety, region, or price, and offers detailed tasting notes to enhance your wine appreciation. On iOS, Android, and Desktop, users can browse wines using its advanced natural language search bar, which can understand prompts of any length or complexity. The app also includes innovative features like scanning multiple wine bottles simultaneously, comparing expert and peer ratings, and creating a personalized wine collection.

Here are ways VinoVoss differs from other wine apps:

Ask the AI-powered Smart Somm your questions
Meet Smart Somm, your personal wine expert who lives in your pocket. VinoVoss' signature Smart Somm takes into account your unique taste, occasion, and budget to suggest the perfect wines, ensuring every choice is a refined selection. Unlike a search engine, Smart Somm can answer any question about wine (no keywords or specific searches needed) and have a conversation with you, just like the knowledgeable and friendly sommelier and your local wine shop or grocer.

Scan multiple bottles at the same time
Our innovative scanning feature allows you to effortlessly scan multiple wine bottles simultaneously, unlike our competitors. Quickly access reviews, ratings, and pairing suggestions instantly, making your shopping experience both efficient and enjoyable.

Discover the aromas and flavors of each wine
Delve into the intricate profiles of each wine, whether the wine has notes of clove, grapefruit, or even leather. Enhance your palate and knowledge with detailed tasting notes that elevate your wine appreciation.

Separate expert and peer ratings
Discover sommeliers' more nuanced evaluations of each wine and compare that to other people's personal ratings. Make the best decision for you, your friends or family with this unique dual rating system.

Find the perfect match for your occasion
From housewarmings to brunch, VinoVoss helps you find the ideal wine to complement your menu. Use our advanced pairing options to ensure your selections are perfectly suited to the occasion, impressing your guests every time.

Curate your unique collection
Create and manage a personalized wine list with ease. VinoVoss lets you track your favorite wines, organize wish lists, and keep a record of your tasting history, ensuring you always have the perfect wine on hand.

Find your new favorites in a store near you
Discover new wines available at local stores. VinoVoss provides you with information on where to purchase your selected wines nearby, making it easy for you to get to uncorking faster.

More ways to upgrade your wine experience with VinoVoss:
- **Learn**: Access a wealth of information about wine regions, grape varieties, and winemaking techniques.
- **Collect and share**: Easily track and review your favorite wines, add them to your virtual cellar or wishlist, and share your favorites with friends.

VinoVoss is a blend of tradition and technology that's reshaping how we interact with one of the world's oldest beverages. Whether you're a novice or a connoisseur, VinoVoss makes finding the ideal wine for any occasion effortless and enjoyable. VinoVoss greatly simplifies wine discovery, exploration and enjoyment of wines of the world. It is a personalized, interactive experience that empowers users to make wine selections with confidence.

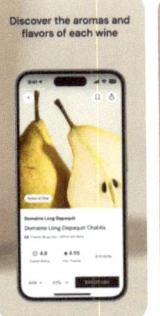
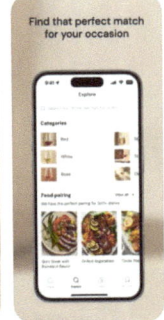

CONNECT WITH MERILEE

SUZE ORMAN:

EMPOWERING FINANCIAL INDEPENDENCE THROUGH KNOWLEDGE AND CONFIDENCE

Suze Orman has long been a guiding force in the world of personal finance, helping millions take control of their financial destinies. With a career spanning decades, Orman's mission has remained steadfast: to empower individuals with the knowledge and confidence to make sound financial decisions. Through her books, television shows, and public speaking, she has demystified financial concepts, making them accessible to the everyday person. Her philosophy is rooted in the belief that financial security is not just about wealth accumulation but about making informed choices that align with one's goals and values.

Orman's journey to financial expertise was unconventional, making her success story all the more inspiring. Born into modest circumstances, she initially worked as a waitress before embarking on a career in finance. Her experiences shaped her approach to money, leading her to develop practical strategies that resonate with a broad audience. She understands firsthand the struggles of financial instability and has dedicated her life to equipping others with the tools to overcome them.

At the core of Orman's teachings is the principle of financial independence. She advocates for smart budgeting, prudent investing, and the importance of an emergency fund. She has repeatedly emphasized that financial freedom is not about how much one earns but how well one manages their money. Her advice is particularly valuable in a world where economic uncertainties can disrupt even the most carefully laid plans. Orman encourages individuals to make financial decisions that provide long-term security rather than short-term gratification.

Beyond her financial expertise, Orman's impact is deeply rooted in her ability to inspire confidence. She does not simply offer advice—she instills a sense of financial self-reliance. Her books, such as The 9 Steps to Financial Freedom and The Money Book for the Young, Fabulous & Broke, have served as essential guides for those looking to build their financial futures. She has also used her platform to advocate for financial literacy among women, recognizing the unique challenges they face in wealth-building. Her straightforward, no-nonsense approach has earned her a loyal following and cemented her status as one of the most influential voices in personal finance.

Orman's contributions align seamlessly with the theme of Success Savvy Magazine's April issue, *"Financial Futures: Empowering Path to Wealth and Success."* Her life's work exemplifies the power of financial knowledge in transforming lives, proving that sustainable wealth-building is within reach for those who are willing to take control of their money. By educating and empowering others, she has played a pivotal role in shaping a future where financial security is not a privilege but a right accessible to all.

GRAB YOUR COPY NOW

WWW.AMAZON.COM/DP/1964619955

Pray, Don't Panic: The Path to Inner Calm offers a powerful collection of stories from women who have transformed fear into faith through prayer and trust. Led by Hanna Olivas and 25 inspiring authors, this book serves as a beacon of hope, showing how faith can guide us through life's toughest moments with grace and resilience.

Each chapter reminds us that choosing prayer over panic fosters inner peace, strength, and a deeper connection with our purpose. More than an anthology, this book is an invitation to embrace faith as the key to a calm and fulfilling life.

SHOP NOW

PUBLISHED BY

BREAKING FINANCIAL CHAINS:

EMPOWERING WOMEN TO REWRITE THEIR MONEY STORIES

BY JAX CRIDER

In a world where financial security is often dictated by outdated rules and rigid systems, many find themselves feeling stuck—despite doing everything *"right."* They budget, save, and follow conventional wisdom, yet financial freedom remains elusive. Women, in particular, often experience the weight of societal expectations, navigating an invisible tightrope between responsibility and autonomy.

I know this struggle firsthand.

When I launched PBJ Mortgage in 2020, I had years of experience in finance, but nothing could have prepared me for the personal and professional storms ahead. A miscarriage, a premature birth, 47 days in the NICU, employees quitting without notice, and a shifting mortgage market all collided in a whirlwind that could have crushed me. But I wasn't just fighting for myself—I was fighting for the women who had trusted me to help them create a financial future on their terms.

That's when I made a pivotal decision: I refused to let financial systems dictate my success. Instead, I set out to rewrite the rules.

From Crisis to Change: The Birth of Financial Mastery Simplified

The financial industry thrives on formulas: Spend less, save more, invest wisely. But what happens when those formulas don't fit your life? What if the conventional path leaves you exhausted, frustrated, and feeling like a failure?

I realized that true financial empowerment isn't about forcing people into a predetermined system—it's about giving them the tools and confidence to create a system that works for them. That's why I built Financial Mastery Simplified, a program designed to help women reset their financial mindset and step into their power.

A Movement, Not Just a Program

At its core, Financial Mastery Simplified isn't just about money—it's about freedom.

It's about amplifying the voices of those who have been told they're *"bad with money"* when the real issue is that they were never given the right framework to succeed. It's about breaking generational cycles, challenging outdated financial advice, and reclaiming control.

Women come to this program feeling stuck. They leave feeling empowered. The journey isn't just about numbers—it's about transformation.

They stop feeling guilty for breaking the *"rules."*
They stop making financial decisions from a place of fear.
They start designing a life where money serves them—not the other way around.

And the ripple effect is undeniable.

When one woman breaks free from financial shame, she teaches her children that wealth is more than just numbers—it's mindset, autonomy, and choice. When she starts making financial decisions rooted in confidence, she inspires her community to do the same. When she amplifies her voice, she lifts others with her.

What's Your Financial Spirit Animal?
Change starts with a decision. A decision to stop playing by rules that don't serve you. A decision to redefine financial success on your terms. A decision to become the hero of your own story.

If you're tired of feeling stuck, know this: You are not broken. The system was never built for you. But you have the power to rebuild it.

The women in Financial Mastery Simplified are proof that transformation is possible. They are the unsung heroes of financial change—rewriting their money stories and, in the process, rewriting the narrative for future generations.

Because when one woman reclaims her financial power, she changes more than just her life—she changes the world.

Curious about your Financial Spirit Animal? If you're wondering which one you are and want to learn more about leveling up your financial game, scan the QR code below!

CONNECT WITH JAX

www.urals.co/jax-crider
www.urals.co/fmscollege
www.facebook.com/jax.crider
www.instagram.com/jax_crider
www.linkedin.com/in/pbj-mortgage-
jacqueline-crider

MELINDA GATES:

CHAMPION OF GLOBAL FINANCIAL EMPOWERMENT

Melinda Gates has spent decades advocating for financial inclusion, gender equality, and economic empowerment on a global scale. As the co-chair of the Bill & Melinda Gates Foundation, she has been instrumental in reshaping the landscape of philanthropy by focusing on initiatives that uplift women and underserved communities. Through strategic investments, innovative programs, and her unwavering commitment to improving financial access, she has played a transformative role in advancing economic opportunities for millions worldwide.

Gates' journey into financial and social advocacy began early in her career. With a background in computer science and economics, she joined Microsoft in the late 1980s and quickly rose through the ranks. During her tenure, she gained firsthand experience in corporate strategy, leadership, and financial management, skills that would later define her philanthropic work. While she could have remained in the corporate world, Gates chose a different path—one that focused on leveraging wealth and resources to create systemic change.

A significant part of her work has centered on financial inclusion for women, particularly in developing nations. Through the Gates Foundation, she has championed programs that provide women with access to digital banking, microloans, and entrepreneurial resources. She recognizes that financial independence is a key factor in gender equality and has worked tirelessly to remove barriers that prevent women from achieving economic security. By funding initiatives that improve financial literacy, access to capital, and technology-driven banking solutions, Gates has empowered women to take control of their economic futures.

One of her most impactful efforts has been her advocacy for women's economic rights on a policy level. She has worked with governments, financial institutions, and global organizations to push for reforms that ensure women have equal access to financial tools. Whether it's advocating for fair wages, improved maternity leave policies, or greater representation of women in leadership roles, Gates understands that true financial empowerment comes from structural change.

Beyond financial inclusion, Gates has also focused on wealth redistribution through philanthropy. She has been a leading voice in the Giving Pledge, an initiative that encourages billionaires to donate a significant portion of their wealth to charitable causes. Her approach to philanthropy is deeply strategic—she believes in not just donating money but investing in sustainable solutions that create long-term economic opportunities. This mindset has led to groundbreaking investments in healthcare, education, and economic development, all of which contribute to financial stability for underserved populations.

In recent years, Gates has become an even more outspoken advocate for women's financial power. In her book, The Moment of Lift, she explores the intersection of financial empowerment and gender equality, making a compelling case for why investing in women leads to stronger economies and more prosperous societies. Her leadership and advocacy continue to inspire new generations of women to seek financial independence, ensuring that wealth is not just accumulated but also used as a tool for positive change.

Gates' work serves as a powerful reminder that financial empowerment is about more than just individual success—it's about creating systems that allow entire communities to thrive. Through her vision, influence, and commitment to economic justice, she has reshaped the conversation around wealth, philanthropy, and financial equality, leaving an enduring impact on the world.

VOIR BY TATIANA
WEDDING FILMS

ABOUT US

At Voir by Tatiana, we understand the profound significance of capturing the magic and emotion of one of life's most cherished moments—your wedding day.
With a blend of creativity, expertise, and state-of-the-art equipment, we specialize in transforming fleeting moments into timeless memories that will be cherished for generations to come.

OUR SERVICES

- Weddings
- Elopements
- Destination Weddings

BOOK NOW

Colorado & Beyond   www.voirvideos.com   contact@voirvideos.com

Book Coming December 2025

Courageous Women: Casting Cares Upon Jesus

By

Carmen K. Maendel

Summary

This book can be summarized in the following way: this is a book that incapsulates the miraculous and wonderful ways that Jesus Christ works in all of our lives. It highlights both my life stories and those of women that were kind enough to share their stories and personal experiences they had with Jesus Christ in this book. This is a beautiful collection of stories that will take you on a range of emotions as you join the journey of each of these courageous women of God. You will see how God takes something that was bad or negative and transforms it into something positive for His glory. These stories are true, raw, emotional, and incredible examples of ways that God guides and directs each of our lives.

Proverbs 16:9 "A man's heart plans his way, But the LORD directs his steps."

Connect with Carmen

https://www.facebook.com/ncmaendel

https://natespropertymaintenance.com

JEWELRY WORN,

THEN REBORN VIA SHOP'S 'LIFETIME BUYBACK PROMISE'

BY MERILEE KERN

Innovative e-Tailer Turns Your Gold into Green Investments

What if your jewelry didn't just shine, but it functioned financially for you, too? Sonalore is an e-Tailer transforming the fine jewelry sector with a *"Lifetime Buyback Promise,"* allowing consumers to sell back their gold jewelry for cash or credit anytime at market value—with just one click. Unlike designer duds that don't trade as a commodity, Sonalore pieces are crafted to appreciate, blending beauty with asset accumulation.

Sonalore jewelry is crafted to be passed down generations, but is designed with freedom and fiscal ingenuity at its core. Choose to cherish your jewelry forever, or sell it back with one click for your choice of cash or store credit anytime you want, calculated based on the stock market value price of gold.

"Gold is beautiful to wear, but also a great investment to keep...be it a gold bar, a stunning bracelet or even a broken chain, each gram of gold is precious," said Sonalore CEO Nidhi Singhvi. *"Unlike designer bag, sneakers and other style staples, gold is traded as an asset across the world and its value increases steadily over the years."*

A Golden Opportunity for Savvy Consumers

- **Sustainable asset-minded shopping.** Sell back your jewelry as easily as you buy it so it can be recycled and reborn with Sonalore's *"lifetime buyback guarantee."* Get instant and fair buyback valuations, so you can refresh your collection anytime. Monitor your jewelry portfolio and see how it grows in value over time. At anytime, sell it back with a click of a button.

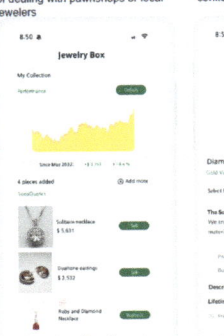
Monitor all your jewelry investments everyday, with no hassle of dealing with pawnshops or local jewelers

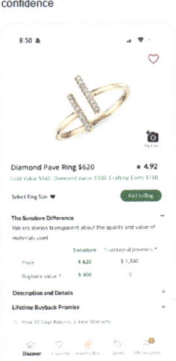
Add to your jewelry investments from our extensive collection with confidence

Sell Back to your sonalore jewelry, knowing the value in transparent way

Evaluate true value of any jewelry, with just a few simple steps

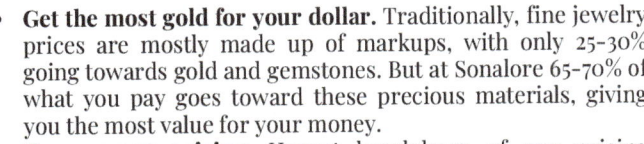

- **Get the most gold for your dollar.** Traditionally, fine jewelry prices are mostly made up of markups, with only 25-30% going towards gold and gemstones. But at Sonalore 65-70% of what you pay goes toward these precious materials, giving you the most value for your money.
- **Transparent pricing.** Honest breakdown of our pricing policies and product details.
- **Ethically made.** Responsibly sourced precious stones and fair wages for our workers.
- **Artisan quality.** Highest quality jewels crafted by global artisans from India to Italy.

"We find the industry pricing standards shockingly unfair," Singhvi continued. *"At Sonalore we reverse the trend. So 65-70% of our prices go towards gold and precious materials, instead of the standard 25-30%. We focus on crafting jewelry with a high value of gold for every dollar you spend. We are proud of our efforts to combine jewelry with building assets, at inspiringly low prices."*

The Sonalore Difference
Same ring, vastly different consumer experiences.

With transparent pricing, ethically sourced materials, and 65-70% of each purchase going directly into gold and gemstones (instead of the egregious industry-standard markups), Sonalore is combining luxury accessories with financial freedom, well-suited for savvy shoppers that appreciate utmost flexibility, sustainability and value.

CONNECT WITH MERILEE

www.TheLuxeList.com
www.SavvyLiving.tv
www.Instagram.com/MerileeKern
www.Twitter.com/MerileeKern
www.Facebook.com/MerileeKernOfficial
www.LinkedIn.com/in/MerileeKern

ABOUT THE AUTHOR:

Merilee Kern, MBA is an internationally-regarded brand strategist and analyst who reports on noteworthy industry change makers, movers, shakers and innovators across all B2B and B2C categories. This includes field experts and thought leaders, brands, products, services, destinations and events. Merilee is Founder, Executive Editor and Producer of *"The Luxe List."* As a prolific business and consumer trends, lifestyle and leisure industry voice of authority and tastemaker, she keeps her finger on the pulse of the marketplace in search of new and innovative must-haves and exemplary experiences at all price points, from the affordable to the extreme—also delving into the minds behind the brands. Her work reaches multi-millions worldwide via broadcast TV (her own shows and copious others on which she appears) as well as a myriad of print and online publications. Some or all of the accommodations(s), experience(s), item(s) and/or service(s) detailed above may have been provided or arranged at no cost to accommodate if this is review editorial, but all opinions expressed are entirely those of Merilee Kern and have not been influenced in any way.

GRAB YOUR COPY NOW

HTTPS://WWW.AMAZON.COM/DP/1964619904

In Women Decision Makers: Women's Stories and Strategies in Decision-Making, Hanna Olivas, Adriana Luna Carlos, and co-authors Jacqueline Long, Tania Vasallo, Nermin Fathy, Megan Waite, and Megan Henry showcase how women are breaking barriers and shaping a more inclusive future. Through powerful stories and strategies, this book highlights the impact of diverse leadership across industries.

A must-read for those passionate about leadership, gender equality, and social change, it inspires action and celebrates the power of women in decision-making.

SALLIE KRAWCHECK:
REDEFINING WEALTH AND LEADERSHIP FOR WOMEN

Sallie Krawcheck has long been a formidable presence in the financial world, breaking barriers in an industry historically dominated by men. As a former Wall Street executive and the founder of Ellevest, a digital investment platform designed specifically for women, she has dedicated her career to promoting financial literacy, investment confidence, and wealth-building opportunities for women. Her leadership has not only transformed financial services but has also challenged traditional notions of power and success in finance.

Krawcheck's career trajectory is marked by both resilience and innovation. She held top positions at some of the world's most prestigious financial firms, including CEO of Merrill Lynch Wealth Management and CFO of Citigroup. In an era when women were vastly underrepresented in executive roles, she navigated corporate finance with a clear vision and a commitment to ethical leadership. Her reputation as *"the most powerful woman on Wall Street"* was built on her ability to drive financial growth while advocating for investor transparency and responsible business practices.

Despite her success in traditional finance, Krawcheck recognized a persistent problem: the investment industry was not serving women effectively. Studies showed that women were less likely to invest than men, often due to a lack of tailored financial guidance. Seeing this gap, she launched Ellevest, an investment platform designed to help women take control of their financial futures. Unlike traditional firms that focused on short-term gains, Ellevest emphasized long-term financial planning, career growth, and life-stage investing, ensuring that women could build sustainable wealth on their own terms.

One of Krawcheck's most significant contributions to financial empowerment is her advocacy for closing the gender wealth gap. While much attention has been given to the gender pay gap, she has highlighted an even greater issue: women's lack of investment participation, which significantly impacts long-term wealth accumulation. Through Ellevest and her broader financial education efforts, she has worked to shift the conversation from simply earning more to strategically growing wealth through investing. She believes that financial independence is the key to broader gender equality, and her work has inspired countless women to take control of their financial destinies.

Krawcheck's insights extend beyond investing. She has been a vocal advocate for financial education in the workplace, urging companies to implement programs that teach women how to negotiate salaries, manage personal wealth, and prepare for retirement. She has also spoken extensively on the importance of women in leadership, arguing that diverse leadership teams make for stronger, more financially resilient companies. Her belief in the power of women's financial empowerment is evident in her book, Own It: The Power of Women at Work, where she outlines strategies for women to succeed in business and finance.

By redefining what financial empowerment looks like for women, Krawcheck is building a future where wealth is no longer a privilege, but a right that every woman can confidently claim.

SHERYL SANDBERG:

A VISIONARY LEADER IN FINANCE AND BUSINESS

Sheryl Sandberg has built a career defined by leadership, resilience, and financial acumen. As the former Chief Operating Officer of Meta (formerly Facebook), she played a crucial role in transforming the company into a global powerhouse, demonstrating her ability to drive revenue growth and financial success. Beyond her corporate achievements, Sandberg has become a leading advocate for women in business, encouraging them to embrace leadership roles and financial independence.

Before joining Facebook in 2008, Sandberg had already established herself as a formidable figure in both finance and technology. She began her career at the World Bank, focusing on economic development, before earning her MBA from Harvard Business School. She later joined Google, where she played a pivotal role in developing its online advertising strategy. Her success at Google made her an attractive candidate for Facebook, where she was tasked with turning the then-young social media platform into a profitable business.

"IF YOU'RE OFFERED A SEAT ON A ROCKET SHIP, DON'T ASK WHAT SEAT! JUST GET ON."

Under Sandberg's leadership, Facebook transformed from a rapidly growing tech company into one of the most influential businesses in the world. She spearheaded the development of its advertising model, which became the backbone of the company's financial success. Her ability to balance strategic innovation with sound financial management helped Facebook generate billions in revenue and establish itself as a dominant force in digital advertising.

Beyond her corporate role, Sandberg has been a powerful advocate for gender equality in the workplace. Her book, Lean In: Women, Work, and the Will to Lead, became a global phenomenon, inspiring women to pursue leadership positions and demand their rightful place at the table. She has spoken extensively about the systemic barriers that hold women back in business, emphasizing the importance of financial independence as a key factor in gender equality.

One of Sandberg's most significant contributions to financial literacy and empowerment has been her focus on encouraging women to take control of their careers and finances. She has argued that economic security gives women greater freedom and influence, both in the workplace and in society. Through her Lean In foundation and advocacy work, she has supported initiatives that help women negotiate better salaries, access leadership opportunities, and gain financial confidence.

Sandberg's career is a testament to the power of combining business strategy with financial intelligence. Her leadership at Meta not only demonstrated her ability to drive financial success but also highlighted her commitment to fostering inclusive workplaces where women can thrive. Even after stepping down from her role as COO, her influence continues to shape conversations around leadership, business growth, and financial empowerment.

Her legacy is one of transformation—both in business and in the way women approach leadership and financial independence. By challenging outdated norms and championing women's advancement in finance and technology, Sandberg has left an indelible mark on the corporate world, proving that financial success and leadership go hand in hand.

3 COMMON MONEY MISTAKES WOMEN MAKE—

AND HOW TO OVERCOME THEM

BY TOLULOPE S. OLANIYAN

Money isn't just about numbers—it's about freedom, choices, and impact. As a qualified financial adviser, transformation coach, and finance professional with a background in economics, I've worked with countless women who feel stuck in their financial journey. I see the same patterns over and over—brilliant, hardworking women struggling with money, not because they lack ambition, but because no one taught them how to take control of their finances and build lasting wealth.

As a Black Irish woman, I understand the unique challenges we face—balancing responsibilities, breaking generational cycles, and navigating financial systems that weren't always designed for us. That's why I'm passionate about helping women shift from financial survival to financial success. I don't just talk about money—I teach, coach, and empower women to thrive beyond borders—because financial freedom is for all of us.

If you've ever felt like money slips through your fingers no matter how hard you work, or you avoid financial conversations out of fear, you're not alone. But today, we're breaking that cycle. Let's talk about three common money mistakes women make and how to fix them—because you deserve financial peace and power.

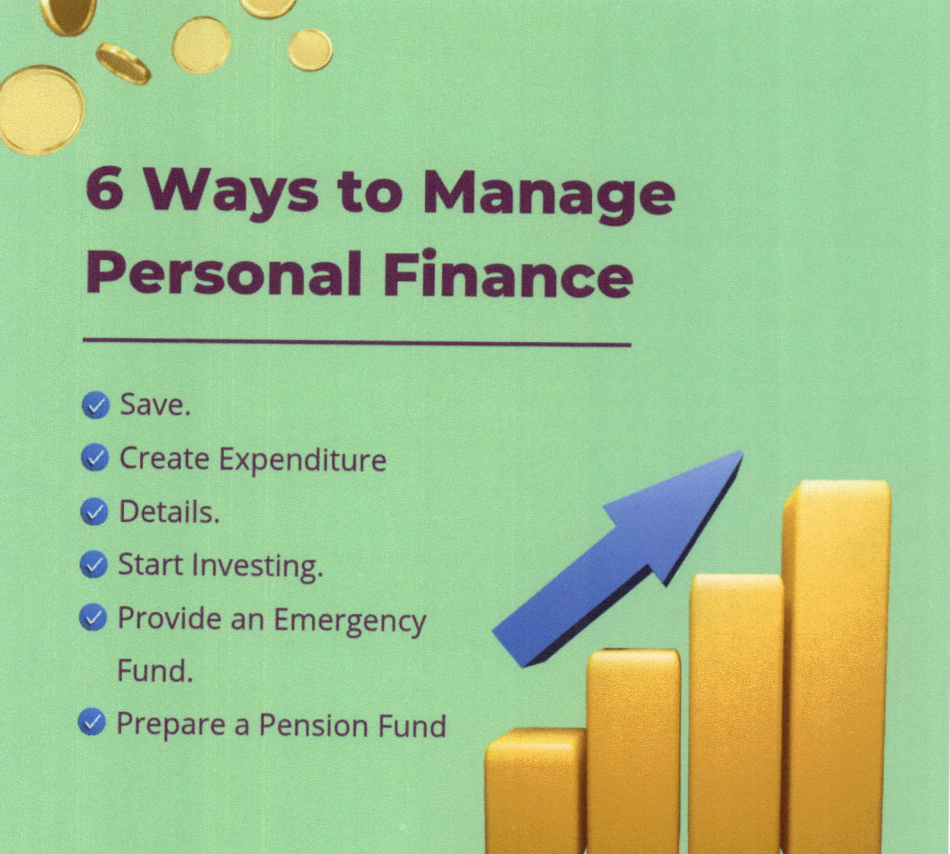

1. Avoiding Money Conversations

Women are amazing at handling responsibilities, but when it comes to discussing money—whether negotiating a salary, setting boundaries, or planning for the future—many of us hesitate. Why? Because we were conditioned to believe money talk is uncomfortable or *"not for us."*

The Cost of This Mistake: Avoiding financial conversations means missing out on opportunities—higher pay, better deals, and smarter financial decisions.

What you can do

- Normalize money talks. Discuss finances openly with your partner, friends, or a mentor. We break cycles by breaking the silence.
- Negotiate with confidence. Whether it's for a raise, business deal, or even household expenses, your financial well-being matters.
- Educate yourself. Take a financial course, join a money mastermind, or work with a coach (like me!) to boost your money confidence.

2. Not Having a Financial Plan

Many women focus on daily expenses but don't think long-term. The result? Living paycheck to paycheck, struggling with debt, or feeling financially stuck. A plan isn't just about saving—it's about building wealth and creating options.

The Cost of This Mistake: Without a plan, it's easy to overspend, under-save, and miss opportunities to grow your wealth.

What you can do:

- Create a budget that fits your life. Forget rigid spreadsheets— use a flexible, personalized system that works for YOU.
- Set clear financial goals. Whether it's buying a home, investing, or retiring early, clarity makes saving and earning easier.
- Build an emergency fund. Aim for 3-6 months of expenses as a safety net. Life happens—be prepared.

3. Relying on One Income Stream

One paycheck? One source of income? That's financial risk. Job loss, economic shifts, or unexpected expenses can shake your financial stability if you don't have a backup plan.

The Cost of This Mistake: No financial cushion means more stress, fewer choices, and a slower path to wealth.

- Diversify your income. Explore side hustles, freelancing, investments, or leveraging your skills for extra cash flow.
- Look into passive income. Rental properties, stocks, digital products, or affiliate marketing can make you money while you sleep.
- Invest in yourself. The best asset? YOU. Take courses, expand your skills, and open doors to higher-paying opportunities.

Take Back Your Financial Power

Women are powerful wealth-builders. The moment we start owning our financial journey, everything changes—more security, more freedom, more impact. And, when women thrive financially, we change the world.

CONNECT WITH TOLULOPE

www.eventaal.com
www.facebook.com/profile.php?id=100015001145314

MARIA SHARAPOVA:
FROM TENNIS CHAMPION TO FINANCIAL POWERHOUSE

Maria Sharapova is known to the world as a fierce competitor on the tennis court, but her success extends far beyond her athletic achievements. As a five-time Grand Slam champion, she dominated the sport with determination and strategic prowess. However, her transition from professional athlete to successful entrepreneur has been just as remarkable. Through savvy investments, brand partnerships, and the creation of her own business empire, Sharapova has proven that financial acumen is as essential to long-term success as talent and discipline.

Sharapova's journey to financial independence began during her tennis career. Born in Russia, she moved to the United States as a child to pursue her dream of becoming a world-class athlete. By the age of 17, she won her first Wimbledon title, launching her into global stardom. But unlike many athletes who focus solely on their sport, Sharapova understood early on the importance of financial planning and business development. She secured lucrative endorsement deals with major brands like Nike, Porsche, and Evian, making her one of the highest-paid female athletes in the world.

What set Sharapova apart was her approach to wealth-building. Instead of merely serving as a brand ambassador, she took an active role in shaping her business ventures. In 2012, she launched Sugarpova, a premium candy brand that quickly expanded into a global success. While many viewed it as an unusual move for an athlete, Sharapova saw it as an opportunity to leverage her brand and build a sustainable business outside of tennis. She was involved in every aspect of the company, from product development to marketing and distribution, ensuring that it reflected her vision of quality and luxury.

Sharapova's entrepreneurial mindset also extended to strategic investments. She wisely diversified her portfolio by investing in promising startups and businesses, including fitness and wellness brands. Her ability to identify emerging trends and align herself with innovative companies demonstrated her keen financial instincts. Unlike many athletes who struggle with financial stability after retirement, Sharapova took control of her economic future by making informed, calculated decisions that would provide long-term security.

Her influence as a businesswoman goes beyond personal success. Sharapova has become an advocate for financial literacy and empowerment, particularly for female athletes and young women looking to break into the business world. She has spoken openly about the importance of understanding financial contracts, negotiating better deals, and taking ownership of one's career beyond a single profession. By sharing her experiences, she encourages others to take an active role in managing their finances, ensuring they are not solely dependent on a single income stream.

Sharapova's story is one of resilience, intelligence, and vision. She has demonstrated that financial success is not just about making money but about making smart choices, diversifying income, and planning for the future. Her ability to transition from a world-class athlete to a powerful business leader serves as an inspiration for anyone looking to take control of their financial destiny. Through discipline, strategic thinking, and an unwavering commitment to excellence, she has built a legacy that extends far beyond the tennis court.

JOIN THE SRS COMMUNITY

WHERE WOMEN RISE TOGETHER!

Connect. Empower. Thrive. Whether you're an entrepreneur, professional, or simply seeking inspiration, **this is your space to grow!**

- Daily Motivation
- Expert Insights
- Sisterhood & Support

You don't have to do it alone—let's rise together!

JOIN NOW!

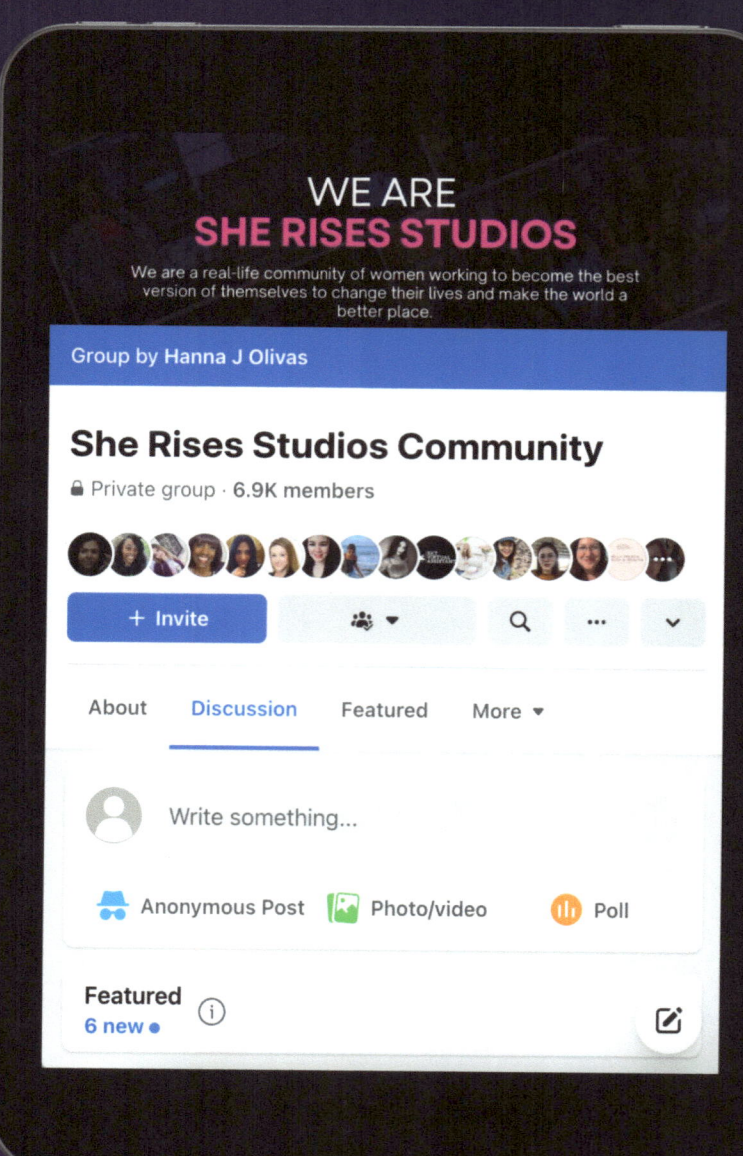

GRAB YOUR COPY NOW

WWW.AMAZON.COM/DP/1964619939

Pray, Live, Lead by Faith: Faith-Fueled Success explores how faith serves as the foundation for success in life, business, family, health, and wealth. Hanna Olivas and co-authors Carmen K. Maendel, Shirley Marie, Erica Elliott, Yalonda Smith, and Ginny Jones share powerful stories of resilience, leadership, and transformation through faith.

This inspiring book, accompanied by a global docuseries, reveals how faith fuels balance, bold decision-making, and lasting success. A must-read for those seeking purpose, strength, and fulfillment in every aspect of life.

amazon.com   **SHOP NOW**

PUBLISHED BY

SHE RISES
STUDIOS

5 APPS FOR SMARTER,

FASTER PROBLEM-SOLVING

BY MERILEE KERN

Today's technology advancements provide unprecedented on-demand assistance, with the variety of services available covering nearly any want and need. From finding the right air fryer recipe or wine to pair with any meal to identifying the perfect contractor for your home improvement project or safeguarding yourself from visual misinformation, there truly is an app for everything. Here are a few noteworthy top picks.

Personalized Wine Selections via the 'VinoVoss AI Sommelier' by BetterAI *(https://vinovoss.com)*

The VinoVoss AI Sommelier app is a revolutionary smartphone app and web-based semantic wine search and recommendation system, developed by BetterAI, is designed to elevate your own wine discovery experience—and that for gift-giving. VinoVoss picks the perfect wine for any occasion courtesy of a highly advanced artificial intelligence architecture. The tool leverages advanced artificial intelligence to act as your personal sommelier, providing tailored wine recommendations based on your unique taste preferences, occasion, and budget. The app's signature feature, Smart Somm, is an AI-powered chatbot trained by world-renowned sommeliers, ready to answer any wine-related questions and guide you to the perfect bottle. The interactive Smart Somm chat intelligently assists in wine exploration, answers questions, and provides educational insight. The database is continually updated and monitored by the VinoVoss team of wine experts and sommeliers to keep up-to-date with today's wine trends. From beginner to seasoned devotee, this search engine is a powerful and streamlined tool to help users build knowledge and shop, sip, and savor. The app also includes innovative features like scanning multiple wine bottles simultaneously, comparing expert and peer ratings, and creating a personalized wine collection. Whether you're a novice or a connoisseur, VinoVoss makes finding the ideal wine for any occasion effortless and enjoyable.

EmpoweredCooks.com Air Fryer Expertise and Recipes *(https://empoweredcooks.com)*

Air fryers Are a staple of modern kitchens, serving up crispy, guilt-free meals with minimal effort—but let's be honest, we've all had a *"learning curve"* moment. Whether it's soggy fries, overcooked chicken, or accidentally setting off the smoke alarm (oops), mastering the air fryer takes a bit of finesse. Enter Cathy Yoder, widely known as the *"Queen of Air Fryers"* with nearly 800,000 followers. From her Empowered Cooks multimedia platform, she offers a free download with her "Top 18 Air Fryer Tips & Tricks along with recommended internal temperatures for meats and baked—all on one page to print to hang on your fridge. For those looking for some meal planning inspiration, Yoder also has a wildly popular cookbook titled *"Easy Air Fryer Recipe Book: Best Airfryer Cookbook Recipes for Beginners to Advanced."* In it, she not only shares delicious air fryer recipes, but also tips and tricks to help you avoid common pitfalls and unlock the full potential of this kitchen marvel—so your next meal is a success. With 35,000 copies sold, this cookbook helps the reader enjoy quick, easy, healthy, crispy and delicious meals with significantly less oil than frying and bake faster than in the oven. Yoder also offers a curated selection of budget-friendly tools and resources on Amazon and through her online store, Pine & Pepper—the eComm arm of Empowered Cooks where she avails an array of video instruction and other resources specific to the joy of air fryer cooking.

Sonalore Jewelry with Buyback Guarantee *(https://sonalore.com)*

What if your jewelry didn't just shine, but it functioned financially for you, too? Sonalore is transforming the fine jewelry sector with a *"Lifetime Buyback Promise,"* allowing consumers to sell back their gold jewelry for cash or credit anytime at market value—with just one click. Unlike designer duds that don't trade as a commodity, Sonalore pieces are crafted to appreciate, blending beauty with asset accumulation. With the company's *"lifetime buyback guarantee,"* you get instant and fair buyback valuations allowing you to refresh your collection anytime—also allowing you to monitor your jewelry portfolio and see how it grows in value over time. Whenever you want, sell it back with a click of a button.

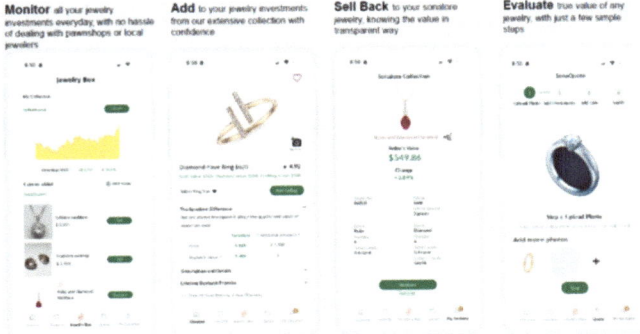

In fact, Sonalore Fine Jewelry's AI-powered platform offers upfront estimates and one click transactability—similar to how other industry technologies can provide instant estimates for a new car or home. Choose to cherish your jewelry forever, or sell it back with one click for your choice of cash or store credit anytime you want, calculated based on the stock market value price of gold. With transparent pricing, ethically sourced materials, and 65-70% of each purchase going directly into gold and gemstones (instead of the egregious industry-standard markups), Sonalore is combining luxury accessories with financial freedom, well-suited for savvy shoppers that appreciate utmost flexibility, sustainability and value.

BitMind Deepfake Detection *(https://bitmind.ai/apps)*

In a world of artificial intelligence, misinformation and fake news, there's no such thing as being too careful. Bitmind offers a sense of security and control over what you see online. The company has developed Numerous free tools that can readily help you identify whether a photo or video you're looking at in the digital realm is real or not. The company's AI Detector App is a simple web page where users can drag-and-drop suspicious images for fast deepfake detection results. Other free apps offered by BitMind include their Chrome Extension flags AI-created content in real-time, while browsin; X Bot that verifies if images on X/Twitter are real or AI-generated; a Discord Bot that erifies if images are real or AI-generated via its Discord Integration; and an AI or Not Game: Fun Telegram bot that tests your ability to distinguish between AI-generated and human-created images. Built by a team of AI engineers hailing from leading tech companies like Amazon, Poshmark, NEAR, and Ledgersafe, BitMind's instant detection of deepfakes helps uphold the credibility of the media, guaranteeing the authenticity of the information we use. A strong deepfake detection enhances digital interactions, supports better decision making and strengthens the integrity of the modern digital world—serving to protect reputations, shield finances and maintain trust for celebrities, politicians, public figures ... and everyone else.

GreatBuildz Homeowner - Contractor Matching Platform *(greatbuildz.com)*

For homeowners, it's critical to hire the best contractor for any sort of home design improvement renovation, repair or build need. All too often, we hear of horror stories that come with hiring shady home contractors who are not honest with their abilities, pricing or other key facets of the vetting and hiring process. The overwhelming amount of online information Further exacerbates the difficulty in finding viable fact checking resources. That's where GreatBuildz.com comes in. Their site makes it easy to match honest home contractors to your specific project. Their chatbot, dubbed *"Katie,"* adds a human touch to navigating the oft maddening world of home modification and maintenance. GreatBuildz.com provides reliable and accurate assistance every step of the way. If you're specifically interested in Accessory Dwelling Units like granny flats, in-law suites, guest houses, casitas and other types of ADUs, the founders of GreatBuildz.com also avail a wealth of tips and information resources at *MaxableSpace.com*—the industry-leading ADU property design / build / construction resource website.

As technology continues to evolve, so too do the innovative solutions that make life easier, safer, and more efficient. From protecting digital integrity and enhancing security with deepfake detection to simplifying home improvement, refining personal taste experiences, optimizing kitchen adventures, and reimagining jewelry as a financial asset, these apps and platforms showcase how technology is shaping modern convenience. By embracing these advancements, users can not only streamline daily tasks but also gain greater confidence in the decisions they make.

In a fast-paced digital age, leveraging the right tools ensures a smarter, more informed, and ultimately more rewarding way of navigating life's many challenges and opportunities.

ABOUT THE AUTHOR:

Merilee Kern, MBA is an internationally-regarded brand strategist and analyst who reports on noteworthy industry change makers, movers, shakers and innovators across all B2B and B2C categories. This includes field experts and thought leaders, brands, products, services, destinations and events. Merilee is Founder, Executive Editor and Producer of *"The Luxe List."* As a prolific business and consumer trends, lifestyle and leisure industry voice of authority and tastemaker, she keeps her finger on the pulse of the marketplace in search of new and innovative must-haves and exemplary experiences at all price points, from the affordable to the extreme—also delving into the minds behind the brands. Her work reaches multi-millions worldwide via broadcast TV (her own shows and copious others on which she appears) as well as a myriad of print and online publications. Some or all of the accommodations(s), experience(s), item(s) and/or service(s) detailed above may have been provided or arranged at no cost to accommodate if this is review editorial, but all opinions expressed are entirely those of Merilee Kern and have not been influenced in any way.

CONNECT WITH MERILEE

www.TheLuxeList.com
www.SavvyLiving.tv
www.Instagram.com/MerileeKern
www.Twitter.com/MerileeKern
www.Facebook.com/MerileeKernOfficial
www.LinkedIn.com/in/MerileeKern

TIM
COOK:

DRIVING FINANCIAL SUCCESS THROUGH INNOVATION AND LEADERSHIP

Tim Cook has redefined corporate leadership and financial strategy through his tenure as the CEO of Apple. Stepping into the role in 2011 after the passing of Steve Jobs, Cook faced the daunting challenge of leading one of the world's most valuable companies while maintaining its legacy of innovation. Under his leadership, Apple not only sustained its dominance but expanded into new markets, achieved record-breaking financial success, and reinforced its status as a global technology powerhouse. His approach to business growth, financial stewardship, and strategic decision-making has cemented his reputation as a visionary executive.

Cook's journey to becoming one of the most influential figures in business began with a strong foundation in operations and financial management. With a background in industrial engineering and an MBA from Duke University, he honed his skills in supply chain logistics and cost efficiency at IBM and Compaq before joining Apple in 1998. His expertise in operations played a crucial role in transforming Apple's supply chain, reducing costs while improving efficiency—key factors in the company's financial resurgence in the early 2000s.

When he assumed the role of CEO, Apple's future was uncertain. Many questioned whether the company could continue its growth without Jobs' visionary leadership. However, Cook quickly proved his ability to steer the company with strategic precision. He prioritized financial stability, expanding Apple's product lines while maintaining a disciplined approach to pricing, investment, and market expansion. His leadership saw Apple diversify its revenue streams beyond the iPhone, launching successful products like the Apple Watch, AirPods, and a suite of subscription-based services, including Apple Music and Apple TV+. This diversification strategy strengthened Apple's financial foundation and ensured its resilience in an ever-changing technological landscape.

One of Cook's most significant financial achievements has been Apple's rise to a multi-trillion-dollar valuation, making it one of the most valuable publicly traded companies in history. His ability to balance innovation with sound financial management has allowed Apple to generate record-breaking revenues while maintaining strong profit margins. Additionally, Cook has been a proponent of returning value to shareholders through stock buybacks and dividends, reinforcing confidence in Apple's long-term financial health.

Beyond financial growth, Cook has emphasized corporate responsibility and sustainability as essential components of Apple's business strategy. He has positioned the company as a leader in environmental sustainability, committing to carbon neutrality and ethical supply chain practices. His belief that financial success should align with social responsibility has set a new standard for corporate governance, proving that profitability and ethical leadership can coexist.

Cook has also used his platform to advocate for financial accessibility and digital inclusion. Through Apple's initiatives, he has championed education programs that provide technology and financial literacy tools to underserved communities, ensuring that technological advancements contribute to broader economic empowerment. His efforts reflect a modern approach to business leadership—one that extends beyond profit generation to creating lasting social impact.

As a leader, Cook exemplifies the power of strategic financial planning, operational efficiency, and long-term vision. His ability to sustain and grow one of the world's most successful companies demonstrates the importance of innovation-driven financial leadership. Through careful decision-making, disciplined investments, and a commitment to ethical business practices, he has secured Apple's place as a global financial and technological leader. His story serves as a testament to how strong financial management and innovative thinking can drive sustained success in an evolving business landscape.

LARGER THAN WORDS:
A WRITER'S JOURNEY OF LOVE, LOSS, AND FINDING HER VOICE

BY MICHELLE SEGUIN

As I went deep within the pain of my loss, I stepped into the sadness and grief and allowed the tears to flow as I wrote to heal deeper than I had before. Writing about my son's passing was excruciating. But in those tears, I found strength. With every word I wrote, I released the pain I had held inside for far too long. And with each release, I began to reclaim my voice.

Finding Your Power Through Writing
When I began writing my book, Larger Than Life: A Mother's Love, Loss, and Her Journey Back to Living, I was scared. I didn't know if I could face the pain I'd buried for so long. But writing wasn't just about putting words on paper; it was about stepping into my power and allowing my truth to surface.

Writing Through the Pain
Writing my book was one of the hardest things I've ever done.

Embracing Your Story
I wasn't afraid that I couldn't write my book. I worried my book wouldn't become the perfect legacy for my son. I worried that our story wouldn't unfold the way I imagined. But as I wrote, I realized that the most powerful thing I could do was be honest, to let my truth flow without forcing it into perfection. Each of us carries a powerful truth within us - a story that has the potential to change lives. When you step into that truth, you step into your power.

Overcoming Fear and Judgment

Fear will try to stop you. It may whisper that your words aren't good enough or your voice doesn't matter. You may worry that others will judge you, misunderstand your pain, or criticize your truth. But at the end of the day, your story is yours. Don't let fear steal your truth. Writing is your act of courage. It is your declaration that you refuse to be silenced.

The Power of Sharing Your Voice

Holding my finished book in my hands for the first time, I knew I had reclaimed my power. I had poured every raw emotion onto those pages: heartbreak, doubt, and love. In doing so, I not only honored my son's memory, I honored myself. The finished product far surpassed my expectations. The healing I experienced through writing my book was profound. I didn't just tell my story; I stepped fully into my strength. I became a woman who could share her pain without shame. I became the woman who refused to let her grief define her.

That same power lives within you. Maybe you've been carrying a story that aches to be told for years. Perhaps you've felt the pull to write but doubted yourself. I'm here to tell you that your words are powerful, and your story can touch lives in ways you can't yet imagine.

Writing your book is an act of self-empowerment. It's a declaration that your truth deserves to be heard. And when you allow your voice to rise, you inspire others to do the same.

Don't wait for the fear to fade. Move forward despite it by stepping through the fear. Let the emotions pour out of you, raw and unfiltered. Write from your truth, and trust your voice is strong enough to carry your story forward.

Your story has the power to change lives, starting with your own. Don't hold back. Stand in your power, pick up your pen, and write the book only you can write.

Your voice is needed. The world is waiting.

CONNECT WITH MICHELLE

www.largerthanlifepublishing.com
www.peacefulconnections.ca
www.facebook.com/largerthanlifepublishing

MELLODY HOBSON:

CHAMPIONING DIVERSITY AND FINANCIAL EMPOWERMENT

"BRAVERY IS NOT THE ABSENCE OF FEAR, IT IS OVERCOMING IT."

Mellody Hobson has emerged as one of the most influential figures in finance, a leader whose work transcends traditional wealth management to address financial literacy and economic inclusion. As Chair of Starbucks and co-CEO of Ariel Investments, she has built a legacy of financial acumen and advocacy, proving that wealth-building is not just about numbers but about access, education, and opportunity. Through her leadership, she has worked to dismantle systemic barriers and empower individuals—particularly those from underrepresented communities—to achieve financial success.

Hobson's journey in finance began with a strong foundation in education and ambition. Raised by a single mother who struggled with financial instability, she witnessed firsthand the consequences of limited financial literacy. These experiences fueled her determination to change the narrative for others. She attended Princeton University, where she honed her skills before joining Ariel Investments, one of the country's largest minority-owned investment firms. Her rise from intern to co-CEO is a testament to her perseverance, intelligence, and unwavering commitment to financial education.

One of Hobson's key contributions to the finance world is her advocacy for diversity in wealth management. She has long emphasized that financial literacy should not be a privilege reserved for a select few but a fundamental right for all. She has worked tirelessly to close the racial wealth gap, encouraging corporate leaders to embrace diversity in both hiring and investment strategies. Her TED Talk, Color Blind or Color Brave?, challenged businesses to confront racial disparities in economic opportunities, making a compelling case for inclusion as a financial imperative.

Her leadership extends beyond investment strategies to real-world financial empowerment. She has been a vocal proponent of early financial education, stressing the importance of teaching children about saving, investing, and credit from a young age. Her belief is that financial security begins with knowledge, and she has dedicated much of her career to ensuring that individuals have the tools to build wealth and break cycles of poverty. She has also played a crucial role in advocating for corporate responsibility, urging companies to invest in communities and foster economic equity.

Hobson's impact aligns perfectly with Success Savvy Magazine's April theme, *"Financial Futures: Empowering Path to Wealth and Success."* Her work exemplifies the power of financial literacy in transforming lives and creating sustainable wealth. She has not only mastered the art of finance but has also leveraged her influence to uplift others. By championing diversity and inclusion, she has reshaped the financial landscape, proving that success is not just about individual wealth but about creating opportunities for all.

FENIX TV

WATCH THE
EMMYS PREMIER EVENT

▶ LIVE ON FENIX TV

FROM BEHIND-THE-SCENES PREP TO OUR
EMMYS WEEK GIFTING SUITE AND THE 76TH
ANNUAL PRIMETIME EMMYS!

www.fenixtv.app

A CONVERSATION WITH THE 'QUEEN OF AIR FRYERS,'
CATHY YODER

BY MERILEE KERN

Widely regarded as the *"Queen of Air Fryers,"* Cathy Yoder—a mother of eight—wanted to prove that air fryers could do more than reheat frozen foods and leftovers. So, she documented her journey on YouTube. Now—with nearly 730,000 subscribers, over 6 million video views and 35,000 cookbooks sold—her channel and thought leadership platform draws over a million monthly visitors, fuels speaking engagements, attracts marquee sponsors, and drives significant affiliate revenue.

As an influencer in the digital marketing world, she has also utilized her experience and knowledge to guide other aspiring bloggers and marketers. She frequently shares valuable insights and strategies that have proven to be instrumental in her own success. With remarkable ingenuity, tenacity, and an uncanny knack for anticipating trends, her viral YouTube videos and influential status within the digital marketing community continue to make her a force to be reckoned with in the world of online content creation.

However, most important to her air fryer empire is that Cathy empowers hundreds of thousands of people to dust off their air fryers and embrace using them to make simple, delicious meals in minutes. With this in mind, and the holiday cooking and gifting season on fast approach, we caught up with Cathy to discuss how she can help make celebratory meals quicker, easier and healthier by using an air fryer as well as the profound success realized through her entrepreneurship, digital marketing and social media influencer endeavors.

Q: You are a mother of eight, and it's been said that you don't like to cook? Is that what made using the air fryer appealing to you?

CY: Yes, that's true. I don't like to cook. But, as a busy mom of eight kids, I needed a way to put food on the table fast--several times a day. I tried meal prep, delivery services, eating out (not good), and more. Nothing worked. Meal prep required too much time in the kitchen. And the other options were too pricey for my deal-seeking nature. That's when I started experimenting with an air fryer—which also appealed to my penchant for new technology. Soon, I discovered I could make simple, delicious, and mostly nutritious meals in minutes. When my kids ate those first dinners without complaining, I had an "aha moment" that dramatically changed how I cook and the trajectory of my business.

In 2020 during the pandemic, with a house full of family members needing to eat, I used my phone to record videos of the food I cooked in the air fryer. The kids tried and rated each recipe. Some even pitched in to help chop, mix, and measure. I posted the videos and recipes on YouTube, and here we are.

I now have a family full of air fryer enthusiasts. The recipe portion of Fabulessly Frugal, which is my original business started to help families save money while enjoying delicious meals, has grown so much that we spun off the cooking content into a site called Empowered Cooks. As a complement to that, I also launched Pine & Pepper, which is a physical product line of cooking accessories. Ironically, my reluctance to cook was an essential ingredient for building this thriving culinary business that helps people (like me) feel more confident in the kitchen.

Q: I understand your Empowered Cooks multimedia platform is designed to guide everyday home cooks on the use of air fryers. What will folks find there?

Some of my most popular videos include *"4 of THE BEST Air Fryers in 2023--And What to AVOID,"* 15 Things You DIDN'T KNOW the Air Fryer Could Make, *"Top 12 AIR FRYER MISTAKES,"* and *"These 15 Recipes Will MAKE YOU WANT an Air Fryer."*

Q: To what do you attribute your book, "Easy Air Fryer Recipe Book: Best Airfryer Cookbook Recipes for Beginners to Advanced," having realized such tremendous success?

CY: Yes, the book project has been such a joy. Inside, readers find more than 150 easy and delicious recipes complete with gorgeous photos. This includes delicious, healthy and effortless meals conveniently organized into six sections: Breakfast, Main Dishes (grouped by protein), Veggies & Sides, Snack & Sandwiches, and Desserts. At the end of the book, you'll find additional quick tips, cheat sheets, conversion charts, and other resources.

Overall, this book is written to transform your air fryer into your all-time favorite kitchen appliance, and teach you how to use your air fryer to create recipes everyone will love. Yummy Air Fryer Recipes isn't full of complicated recipes or crazy ingredients. Each recipe is simple enough for anyone to make, and includes pictures. Plus, the index is arranged to help you quickly find recipes in different categories and ingredients so that you can easily use items you already have on hand in your fridge or your pantry.

If you want to up-level what you make in your air fryer, Yummy Air Fryer Recipes is the cookbook recipe book providing simple-to-follow recipe guidelines getting you top notch results every single time.

Q: You mentioned that you also offer kitchen accessories and resources—what's available for sale?

CY: Through our Pine & Pepper online eCommerce store that's linked with Empowered Cooks, we offer nearly 30 helpful tools, books and recipe resources—some available for as little as 99 cents—to help users make air frying simple, accessible and to get food on the table fast. One of my favorites is a handy magnetic air fryer cheat sheet, which is designed to help prevent overcooked food, helping users cook over 85 foods to perfection. There are also gadgets like the Mistifi 6-ounce Oil Spray Bottle; Premium Air Fryer Liners Premium Air Fryer Liners and an Instant Read Food Thermometer.

And, of course, there is the paperback cookbook as well as a wide range of general and specialized digital recipes books—all under $8—available for immediate download. From protein-focused, dessert, kid-friendly, pizza pleasers and meals for two, to diabetic, gluten-free, vegetarian and dairy-free recipe books, we have something for everyone.

For those who really want to dig in, there's also my *"Air Fryers Unleashed! Digital Course"* as well as the *"Cooking with Cathy"* 6-month subscription.

Q: What does the *"Cooking with Cathy"* 6-month subscription entail?

CY: This is a really exciting, immersive option that provides 6-Months of live online cooking classes designed to help participants make fast, delicious, and easy air fryer meals in the comfort of their own kitchen. It's about so much more than just following a recipe; it's about having a group of people to share it with.

CY: At Empowered Cooks online, my *"Air Fryer Recipes"* cookbook filled with over 150 recipes is available. To date, it has sold over 35,000 copies worldwide, giving folks the confidence and inspiration to enjoy all that an air fryer has to offer. Other resources on the EmpoweredCooks.com platform include access to an air fryer cooking catalog with over 300 video recipes, accessories, a transformative video course, and interactive cooking class sessions where new and experienced air fryer enthusiasts gather with me to cook and chat as we air fry foods in real time! Overall, this platform motivated home cooks to learn the basics of air frying and feel empowered to experiment with more recipes as they progress with the appliance.

Q: Also a prolific social media influencer, your YouTube channel, itself, boasts over 730,000 subscribers. What resources to you provide there?

CY: On my YouTube channel users will find endless air fryer inspiration! I share easy, delicious ways to make the most of your air fryer. With it, I'm on a mission to empower everyday cooks like me to feel more confident in the kitchen. With simple ingredients and easy-to-follow instructions, every air fryer recipe on this channel will help you make delicious, and mostly nutritious, air fryer meals in minutes. We make recipes ranging from amazing air fryer chicken to salmon, steak, veggies, baked goods, and desserts in a fraction of the time it normally takes.

Our *"Cooking with Cathy Community"* allows users to actively participate, learn, ask questions and get premium support when needed. The format is an online Zoom class with recipe cards to print at home. The subscription provides a monthly live cooking show plus access to past recorded shows.

Q: I believe Fabulessly Frugal has an app as well. Tell us about that.

CY: Yes, shopping smart has never been easier. The Fabulessly Frugal app is a mobile database of the best online deals available. Users get deal alerts when you select your favorite brands, shopping categories, or products. And you get access to a price comparison tool that ensures you never fall for *"marketing math tricks"* again.

Q: You had published findings from a survey you conducted unveiling insights into air fryer enthusiasts' preferences—what did you glean from that?

CY: The insights gained from that survey, conducted among our audience of nearly 650,000 subscribers, were compelling, with participants representing a diverse audience demographic. This ranged from empty nesters to a growing cohort of younger enthusiasts between their teens and mid-20s. Among the findings, the survey revealed that owning an air fryer led to faster and more efficient cooking for well over half (67.8%) of users, a shift towards healthier cooking for 44.5%, and increased culinary experimentation for 43%. The usage pattern indicated that 39.7% utilize the air fryer several times a week, 36% use it daily or almost daily, and 9.6% use it once a week. It's been amazing to get these survey results. The insights are opening up new ways for us to support our air fryer community. It's pretty cool to think that air fryers, once just a gadget for zapping frozen foods, have become a kitchen game-changer. We're here to keep bringing everyday cooks the best tips, recipes, and advice, whether they're just starting with an air fryer or have been experimenting with it for a while. It's awesome to be part of the journey with this fantastic kitchen innovation.

In all, Cathy and her multi-faceted Empowered Cooks and Pine & Pepper platforms are bringing the delight of air frying to countless kitchens—and her overarching business insights are inspiring other aspiring entrepreneurs. She's thoughtfully curated a collection of high-quality kitchen tools and recipe books designed to help you prepare air fryer meals quickly and easily, without sacrificing flavor or quality.

In all, Cathy's endeavors are making every day air fryer cooking fun and accessible for everyone, transforming kitchens in a place of joy and creativity.

CONNECT WITH MERILEE

www.TheLuxeList.com
www.SavvyLiving.tv
www.Instagram.com/MerileeKern
www.Twitter.com/MerileeKern
www.Facebook.com/MerileeKernOfficial
www.LinkedIn.com/in/MerileeKern

ABOUT THE AUTHOR:

Merilee Kern, MBA is an internationally-regarded brand strategist and analyst who reports on noteworthy industry change makers, movers, shakers and innovators across all B2B and B2C categories. This includes field experts and thought leaders, brands, products, services, destinations and events. Merilee is Founder, Executive Editor and Producer of *"The Luxe List."* As a prolific business and consumer trends, lifestyle and leisure industry voice of authority and tastemaker, she keeps her finger on the pulse of the marketplace in search of new and innovative must-haves and exemplary experiences at all price points, from the affordable to the extreme—also delving into the minds behind the brands. Her work reaches multi-millions worldwide via broadcast TV (her own shows and copious others on which she appears) as well as a myriad of print and online publications. Some or all of the accommodations(s), experience(s), item(s) and/or service(s) detailed above may have been provided or arranged at no cost to accommodate if this is review editorial, but all opinions expressed are entirely those of Merilee Kern and have not been influenced in any way.

NIKITA KHANDHERIA:
A VISIONARY ENTREPRENEUR TRANSFORMING THE HOSPITALITY INDUSTRY

Born in Marin County and raised in India, Nikita Khandheria is a trailblazing entrepreneur redefining success in the hospitality and food industry. Her journey is one of resilience, adaptability, and relentless ambition.

From a young age, Nikita faced unique challenges—adapting to writing with her right hand despite being left-handed and navigating life in a country where she initially didn't speak the language. Undeterred, she became fluent in five Indian languages and ambidextrous, showcasing her adaptability and determination.

At just 12 years old, she spearheaded a transformative social initiative in rural India, securing a license to perform health exams for women. Beyond medical care, she taught them economic skills, fostering independence and establishing clinics for various treatments. This early experience highlighted her innate leadership and deep commitment to social impact.

Returning to the U.S. at 15, Nikita immersed herself in dependency law, advocating for families. By 16, she was presenting cases in court, demonstrating remarkable maturity and skill. She later pursued a double-degree program, earning degrees in Economics and Mathematics from St. Andrews in Scotland and Computer Science from William & Mary in Virginia, graduating in the summer of 2024.

Before starting university, a serendipitous moment changed her trajectory—she accidentally walked into a business meeting and, seizing the opportunity, pitched a unique hospitality concept to the Kaithans, prominent Indian business leaders. Her boldness and vision convinced them to let her lead the project, ultimately bringing Ditas, her waterfront restaurant in Sausalito, to life.

Nikita launched Ditas in June 2023 while still in school, balancing the demands of running a business with weekly flights to complete her final year. Ditas quickly became more than just a restaurant—it evolved into a social hub for entrepreneurs, business leaders, and young professionals, hosting exclusive dinner parties and networking events. To ensure profitability, she transformed Ditas into a production space for brands like Mollie Stone's, making it profitable from its first month and consistently so thereafter.

Upon graduating, Nikita bought out her investors and realized that Ditas was evolving into something much bigger than a traditional restaurant. With demand for private events soaring—leaving only a handful of nights open for regular dinner service—she decided to pivot. Rather than continue advertising dinner while primarily operating as an event venue, she rebranded under her existing company, Eria. This transition led to Eria Café, offering fresh, clean-label food with a focus on gluten-free and better-for-you products, and Eria Events, a premier event space hosting large-scale, high-end gatherings. The shift has been a massive success, solidifying Eria as a leader in curated dining experiences.

Beyond the event space, Nikita is expanding Eria into national distribution. Her company now supplies over 400 stores in the Bay Area, providing everything from its signature vegan bread to gluten-free pastries and meal plans. She is dedicated to making high-quality, preservative-free food accessible at scale, touching lives through cleaner, more transparent eating.

At just 22 years old, Nikita sits on the boards of multiple startups, including Troora Magazine. Her story is a testament to innovation, resilience, and an unwavering commitment to building sustainable, profitable businesses—all while reshaping the future of hospitality and food.

CONNECT WITH NIKITA

@nikitalyssa
www.eria.co/nikita

RUTH BADER GINSBURG:

A LEGACY OF FINANCIAL EMPOWERMENT FOR WOMEN

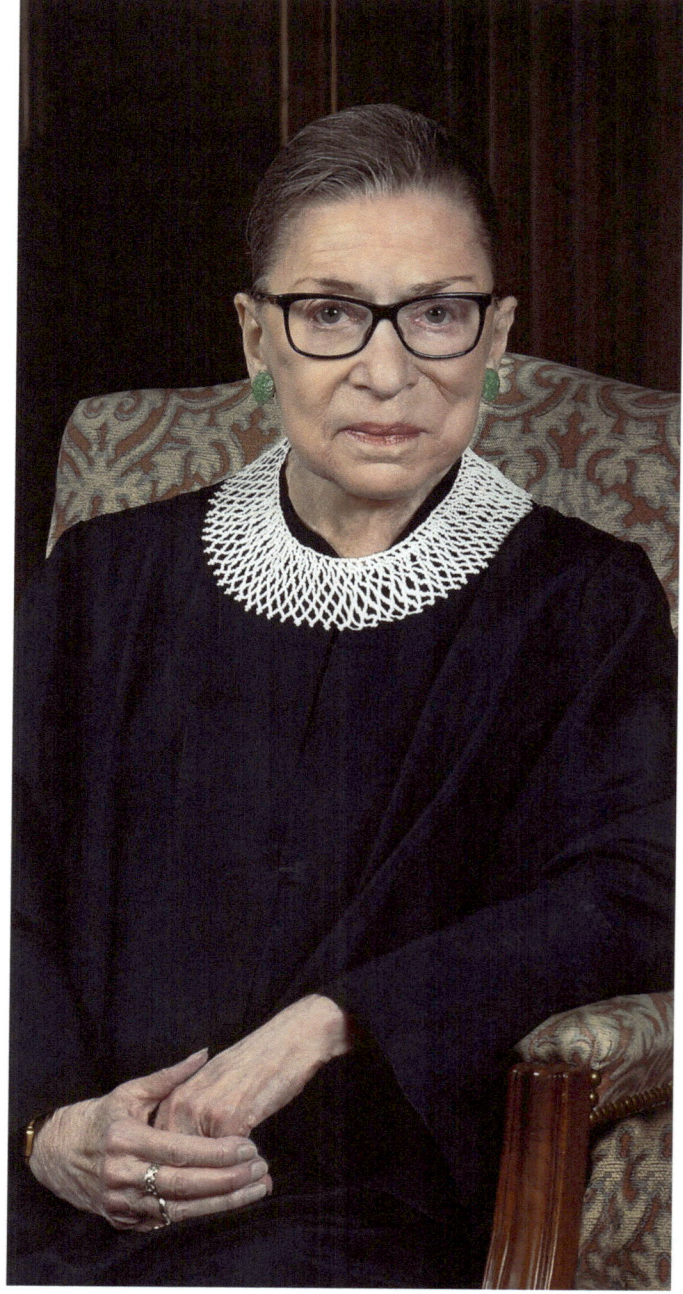

Ruth Bader Ginsburg's legacy as a U.S. Supreme Court Justice is widely recognized for its profound impact on gender equality, but her contributions to financial empowerment are equally significant. Throughout her career, she dismantled legal barriers that had long restricted women's access to financial independence, paving the way for a more equitable economic landscape. Her work reshaped the legal framework surrounding credit, banking, and employment rights, ensuring that women had the same financial opportunities as men.

Ginsburg's legal battles began long before her appointment to the Supreme Court. In the 1970s, she co-founded the Women's Rights Project at the American Civil Liberties Union (ACLU), where she argued and won several landmark cases that directly influenced women's financial rights. One of the most pivotal cases she worked on was *Reed v. Reed* (1971), in which the Supreme Court ruled for the first time that gender-based discrimination violated the Equal Protection Clause of the U.S. Constitution. This decision laid the groundwork for future rulings that ensured women could make financial decisions without male oversight.

One of Ginsburg's most significant contributions to financial equality came in the case of *Frontiero v. Richardson* (1973), where she argued against laws that granted financial benefits to male service members while denying them to female counterparts. Her argument underscored the economic disadvantages that women faced due to discriminatory policies, ultimately leading to greater financial autonomy for women in the military and beyond. Ginsburg's work helped eliminate archaic laws that had long kept women financially dependent, including those that required a male cosigner for loans and mortgages.

Her influence extended beyond the courtroom. Ginsburg was a steadfast advocate for equal pay, recognizing that financial independence was crucial for true gender equality. She was instrumental in shaping the *Lilly Ledbetter Fair Pay Act* of 2009, which made it easier for employees—especially women—to challenge wage discrimination. She believed that financial security was not just about earning money but about having the legal rights to protect one's earnings, invest freely, and build long-term wealth.

Ginsburg's impact is deeply connected to Success Savvy Magazine's April theme, *"Financial Futures: Empowering Path to Wealth and Success."* Her work ensured that women had the legal protections necessary to achieve financial independence, laying the foundation for future generations to build wealth without systemic barriers. Her legacy is a reminder that financial empowerment is not just about individual success but about creating a society where economic opportunities are available to all, regardless of gender. Through her relentless pursuit of justice, Ginsburg transformed financial rights for women, proving that legal equality and financial freedom are inextricably linked.

GRAB YOUR COPY NOW

WWW.AMAZON.COM/DP/1964619963

The Ultimate Wedding Guide: Expert Tips and Secrets for Your Dream Wedding takes the stress out of wedding planning with expert advice from top industry professionals. Hanna Olivas and co-authors Denise O'Malley, Kenya E. Aissa MS, Ashley McCombs, Candice Damele, Kristin Sullivan, Heather Arra, Callie Rackley Carr, Jean Neuhart, and Beverly Little share invaluable insights on budgeting, timelines, vendor selection, and personalized details to make your day unforgettable.

With real-life anecdotes, creative ideas, and step-by-step guidance, this essential resource helps you plan a seamless, joyful celebration.

PUBLISHED BY

MULTIGENERATIONAL AUTHORS:

WEAVING THREADS OF EXPERIENCE INTO LITERATURE

BY ALLISTAR BANKS

A multigenerational author isn't simply one who writes about different age groups. Instead, their work reflects a deep engagement with the interconnectedness of generations. This can manifest in several ways:

- **Historical Context:** Authors may embed their work within a specific historical period, tracing how events and societal norms have shaped the lives of different generations within a family or community.
- **Family Histories:** The author might draw on their own family history, using it as a foundation for exploring the impact of tradition, trauma, and change across generations.
- **Personal Development:** The author's own journey through life, including their relationship with their parents, grandparents, and other relatives, can form the narrative core.
- **Sociocultural Shifts:** The author might explore how societal changes, such as technological advancements, political movements, or economic shifts, influence multiple generations.

Motivations Behind Multigenerational Storytelling

The motivations behind choosing a multigenerational approach are multifaceted:

- **Exploring Family Dynamics:** Authors often use their stories to explore complex family relationships, including love, loss, conflict, and reconciliation across generations. This can involve examining the legacy of past choices and how they impact future generations.
- **Addressing Historical Trauma:** Authors may use multigenerational narratives to address historical injustices and their enduring impact on families. This approach can be seen in works that grapple with the lasting effects of slavery, war, or other forms of oppression.
- **Examining Societal Change:** Tracing the lives of multiple generations allows authors to depict the evolution of societal values, norms, and beliefs. They can illustrate the impact of progress, stagnation, or regression on individuals and families.
- **Personal Reflection:** The process of writing about multiple generations can be a deeply personal one, allowing authors to grapple with their own identity and place within their family's history.

Challenges of Multigenerational Storytelling

While rewarding, writing multigenerational stories presents unique challenges:

- **Research and Accuracy:** Maintaining historical accuracy and representing diverse perspectives within each generation requires significant research and a commitment to authenticity.
- **Balancing Multiple Voices:** Creating believable and distinct voices for each generation requires careful consideration of their individual experiences and perspectives.
- **Avoiding Stereotyping:** Authors must avoid perpetuating harmful stereotypes or generalizations about any particular generation.
- **Emotional Complexity:** Navigating the emotional complexities of familial relationships across time and circumstance can be emotionally demanding.

Case Studies: Illustrative Examples

Several acclaimed authors have masterfully employed the multigenerational approach. For instance, Toni Morrison's *Beloved* explores the enduring trauma of slavery across generations. Similarly, *The House on Mango Street* by Sandra Cisneros portrays the experiences of a young Latina girl within the context of her family's history and community.

These works demonstrate how multigenerational narratives can be powerful tools for examining social and historical issues.

Another compelling example is *"The Remains of the Day"* by Kazuo Ishiguro, which chronicles the life of a butler through the lens of his family's history and the societal changes in England. The novel delves into the impact of class, war, and personal choices across generations.

The Impact and Significance of Multigenerational Narratives

Multigenerational stories offer a unique perspective, providing readers with a richer understanding of human experience. They:

- **Foster Empathy:** By showcasing the interconnectedness of lives across time, such narratives cultivate empathy for individuals and families navigating different circumstances.
- **Challenge Assumptions:** These stories often challenge readers' preconceived notions about particular generations or historical periods, encouraging critical thinking and a deeper understanding of context.
- **Promote Understanding:** By exploring the impact of societal changes, multigenerational narratives can promote a greater understanding of the forces that shape individuals and families over time.
- **Preserve Cultural Heritage:** These narratives can serve as important vehicles for preserving cultural traditions and family histories for future generations.

Conclusion

Multigenerational storytelling is a powerful literary technique that allows authors to explore the complexities of family dynamics, historical events, and societal shifts. By intertwining the threads of experience across generations, these narratives offer profound insights into the human condition. The challenges of research, balancing multiple voices, and avoiding stereotypes are significant, but the potential rewards in terms of empathy, understanding, and cultural preservation are equally significant. These stories serve as a vital reminder of the interconnectedness of past, present, and future, enriching our understanding of ourselves and the world around us.

CONNECT WITH ALLISTAR

www.Facebok.com/AllistarAuthor
www.Instagram.com/allistarthewriter
www.TikTok.com/allistarthewriter

WARREN BUFFETT:

THE ORACLE OF OMAHA AND HIS TIMELESS FINANCIAL WISDOM

Warren Buffett is widely regarded as one of the greatest investors of all time. With a career spanning over seven decades, his financial philosophy has shaped the way individuals and businesses think about wealth, investments, and long-term financial success. As the chairman and CEO of Berkshire Hathaway, Buffett has built an empire through disciplined investing, patience, and a deep understanding of market fundamentals. His journey from a young stock market enthusiast to one of the richest individuals in the world is a testament to the power of strategic financial planning and unwavering principles.

Buffett's fascination with finance began at an early age. As a child, he displayed an extraordinary ability to understand money, making his first stock market investment at just 11 years old. He was influenced by the teachings of Benjamin Graham, a pioneer of value investing, which emphasizes buying undervalued companies with strong fundamentals and holding onto them for long-term gains. This investment philosophy became the cornerstone of Buffett's strategy and set him apart from short-term speculators focused on quick profits.

His approach to wealth-building is rooted in patience and consistency. Buffett has often emphasized that financial success is not about chasing trends but about making well-informed decisions based on intrinsic value. Under his leadership, Berkshire Hathaway evolved from a struggling textile company into a multinational conglomerate, owning major stakes in companies like Apple, Coca-Cola, American Express, and Geico. His ability to identify businesses with sustainable growth potential has allowed him to amass one of the largest fortunes in history while maintaining a reputation for integrity and humility.

Despite his immense wealth, Buffett is known for his frugality and disciplined financial habits. He has famously lived in the same modest home in Omaha, Nebraska, for decades and avoids extravagant spending.

His philosophy underscores the idea that financial security is not about how much one earns but how wisely one manages money. He has consistently advised individuals to prioritize saving, invest in low-cost index funds, and focus on long-term financial growth rather than short-term market fluctuations.

Beyond his personal investment success, Buffett has become a leading advocate for financial literacy and responsible wealth management. He believes that financial education should be accessible to all, emphasizing the importance of understanding compound interest, avoiding unnecessary debt, and making informed financial decisions. His annual shareholder letters have become legendary for their insightful yet straightforward lessons on money, providing guidance to both seasoned investors and everyday individuals looking to build financial stability.

Buffett's legacy extends beyond investing; his commitment to philanthropy has set a new standard for wealth distribution. Through the Giving Pledge, which he co-founded with Bill and Melinda Gates, he has pledged to donate the majority of his fortune to charitable causes, focusing on education, healthcare, and poverty alleviation. His belief that wealth should be used to improve society reflects his broader perspective on financial success—not just as a means of personal gain, but as a tool for meaningful impact.

"BIG OPPORTUNITIES COME INFREQUENTLY. WHEN IT'S RAINING GOLD, REACH FOR A BUCKET, NOT A THIMBLE."

Buffett's influence on financial strategy and wealth-building remains unparalleled. His disciplined approach, emphasis on long-term investing, and commitment to financial education continue to inspire individuals worldwide. Through his actions and teachings, he has demonstrated that true financial mastery is not about chasing riches but about making thoughtful, informed decisions that create lasting prosperity.

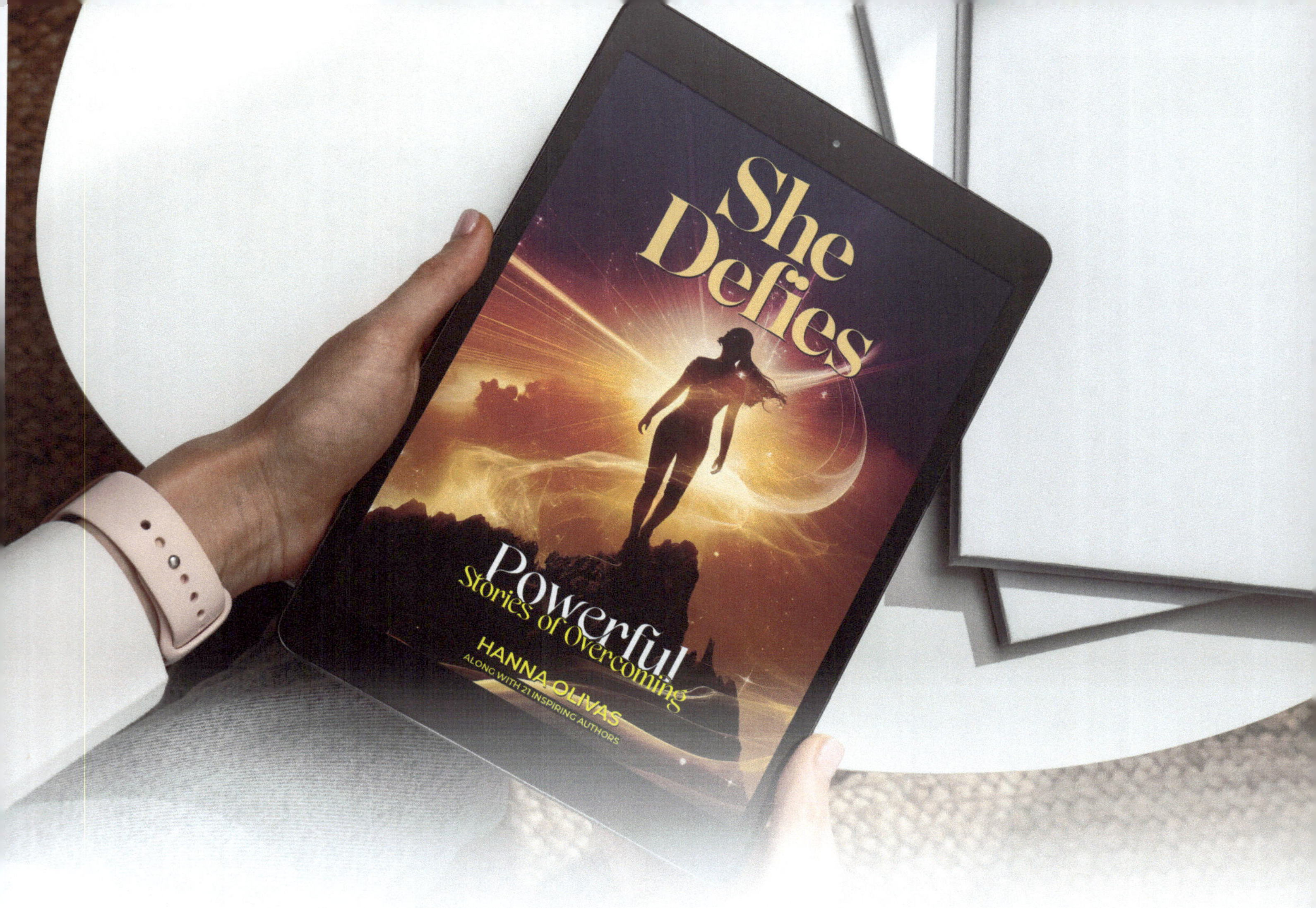

GRAB YOUR COPY NOW

WWW.AMAZON.COM/DP/1966798040

She Defies: Powerful Stories of Overcoming shares the raw, real journeys of 30 extraordinary women who have faced life's toughest challenges and emerged victorious. Led by Hanna Olivas and 21 inspiring authors, this book is a testament to the resilience, courage, and determination found within every woman. Through stories of perseverance —from overcoming personal loss to defying societal expectations—each chapter offers inspiration and strength.

A must-read for anyone seeking empowerment, She Defies reminds us that no matter what life throws our way, we all have the power to rise, overcome, and shine.

PUBLISHED BY

SHE RISES
STUDIOS

FENIX TV

YOUR PLATFORM, YOUR VOICE, YOUR POWER!

Step into the Spotlight as a Host on FENIX TV!

Are you ready to amplify your message, inspire others, and be part of a groundbreaking network dedicated to **empowering women worldwide**? FENIX TV is your platform to **shine as a host**, share your expertise, and connect with a global audience.

WHY HOST ON FENIX TV?

- Reach a worldwide audience passionate about empowerment
- Showcase your voice, brand, and expertise
- Join a community of inspiring leaders and changemakers
- Be part of a network that uplifts and celebrates women

Whether you dream of leading a talk show, sharing powerful stories, or educating and inspiring others—FENIX TV is where your voice matters!

SPOTS ARE LIMITED!

Secure your hosting opportunity today.

 Contact us now at
info@fenixtv.app

 Learn more at
https://fenixtv.app

NETWORKING WITH PURPOSE:
LEVERAGING YOUR TALENTS TO BUILD MEANINGFUL CONNECTIONS

BY MICHELE GUNN

Networking is defined as *"the action or process of interacting with others to exchange information and develop professional or social contacts."* It can and should be done in person, but you also have the option to network virtually. A combination of both would be ideal to truly grow your network

Gone are the days of just meeting people and collecting business cards in the hopes of acquiring new clients. Networking today is about mutual growth and connection, truly building relationships. Remember that every person has unique talents that can enhance their networking success. Utilizing your unique talents will help you stand out in the crowd and discover how to create a positive, lasting impression.

Recognizing and Leveraging Your Talents for Networking
Knowing your strengths and how they can serve others is a key part of self-awareness. Your natural abilities can make networking easier. Take inventory of your natural talents. Is communication, problem-solving, creativity, or recognizing how things are connected part of your innate talents? Leverage your talents to make a connection and build a relationship.

TIP: If you are not sure what talents you possess to leverage in networking, consider taking a strengths assessment (like CliftonStrengths) to identify your top talents. You can also invest in a coach to help you aim those talents.

Building Authentic Relationships, Not Just Contacts
Focus on quality over quantity in networking. It doesn't matter how many contacts you have if there are no relationships. People do business with people they know, like and trust. Those three attributes are based on a relationship, not collecting contact information. When you ask questions and listen, you can determine the best way to offer value to others first.

TIP: Practice active listening and find one way to support each new connection.

The Benefits of Networking for Personal and Professional Success
Networking has been traditionally viewed as an activity for professional growth. In reality, it also offers opportunities for personal growth. You can gain new perspectives, confidence, and lifelong friendships. Professional opportunities include career advancement, mentorship, collaborations and business growth. Ensure you are building relationships in alignment with integrity and service.

TIP: When meeting new people, keep an open mind to the kind of connection and relationship that could be built.

Practical Networking Strategies for Success

Be intentional in your networking strategies. Set goals such as who you want to meet and why. Keep in mind what you have to offer other people. Prepare a strong introduction by perfecting your elevator pitch with authenticity. Don't focus on the sale. Focus on the value you provide. Always follow up by sending a message, a connection request on LinkedIn, or set a future meeting. Give before you receive. Share resources, offer help, and create value. Asking questions will help you determine how to best be of value.

Strengthening Your Networking Skills

Practice sharing who you are in a compelling and authentic way. Attend small networking events to improve your confidence. Many times, virtual networking can be less intimidating. They may be a great place to build confidence.

TIP: Challenge yourself to connect with one new person each week.

Create a Networking Plan

Remember that networking isn't just about making connections. It's about cultivating relationships. Use your talents to connect with confidence and purpose. Plan on attending events and even joining a networking group. If you have not yet considered She Wins Women's Network, take a look. Membership includes in-person as well as virtual networking events. Check it out at www.michelegunn.com/houstonshewinswomensnetwork. When she wins, you win, we all win!

CONNECT WITH MICHELE

www.michelegunn.om
www.facebook.com/michele.jonasgunn
www.linkedin.com/in/michelegunn
www.instagram.com/michelegunn1

10 TOTALLY DOABLE WAYS

SELLERS CAN RAISE RESALE VALUE

BY MERILEE KERN

As the market slowly cools off, homeowners are more interested than ever in finding ways to make sure their properties resell for as much as possible. However, choosing between the many potential renovations makes moving forward with your home improvement and listing for sale overwhelming.

What type of renovations can increase home resale value... or generally add tremendous appeal that can tip the scales in your favor?

Below Jon Grishpul, Co-CEO of www.GreatBuildz.com—a free service that matches homeowners with reliable, pre-screened general contractors—suggests these 10 ways to renovate in intelligent, efficient ways that will help you get more money back as you put your home on the market.

#1: OUTDOOR UPGRADES

Curb appeal cannot be understated, and buyers like to have a group area to come home to. This includes the front yard, back yard, any patio space, and even the driveway. If any of these structures need serious renovation or repair, consider prioritizing this area to increase home value.

Driveways, in particular, can add a lot of value. This is particularly true if you have an unpaved driveway or can expand the driveway to be wider. These will not only add value, but they will also attract attention. Another addition that can make a huge difference is an outdoor living area, such as a deck or patio. Homeowners have found that they get nearly 100% back on this investment, so it can be a great way to enjoy the outdoors and then increase your resale value down the line.

When doing large landscaping and paving projects, however, keep in mind that you should not DIY these renovations unless you have experience with these projects. Hiring a professional to lead with these tasks will be more expensive, but the end results will be far more successful.

#2: OUTDOOR SHOWERS

Thanks to celebrities and popular architects, outdoor showers are having a moment this year as a major remodeling trend.

They're practical outdoor remodeling projects that serve multiple purposes and add unique designs to traditional neighborhoods. You could use your shower to rinse off after swimming in your pool or mowing your lawn. Wash your dog in your outdoor shower to minimize the inevitable indoor mess. They're also great additions to coastal rental homes for guests who frequently jump into the waves. If you're considering an outdoor shower, remember to select features like water-resistant tiles to make it last longer. It should also have complete privacy from any neighbors and drainage that directs water away from your home's foundation.

#3: BUILT-IN BOOKSHELVES

Wobbly bookshelves and temporary furniture are old news. People are looking forward to installing built-in bookshelves this year instead. They add value to any property and give it instant character — built-in shelves are more of a bold statement than standing shelves. They're also a fun opportunity to create a secret doorway or an entertainment cabinet – talk about a fun remodeling trend.

#4: FIREPLACE ADDITION

Many buyers are looking for homes that have charming and warm fireplaces in their homes, and they're not always a common feature. Depending on the layout of your home, it can cost just a few thousand dollars to do this renovation.

Even though the investment is small, the return that you might see when reselling is huge. Plus, it will help your home stand out from others that don't have comparable features. This is a definite must if comparable homes in your area all have fireplaces. Without one, you might miss out on great potential buyers.

#5: EXPANSIVE WINDOWS

Wider windows are popular for numerous reasons. They let more sunlight into your home, decreasing the need for lamps and more electricity. Big windows can also make rooms appear bigger. Your home will feel brand new with a slightly more expansive view of your backyard or neighborhood.

#6: TANKLESS WATER HEATERS

Instead of consuming electricity to continuously heat a large tank of water for small usages, tankless heaters warm water only when you need it. They're more cost-efficient for long-term use than water tanks because you'll use much less daily electricity.

#7: HIDDEN TV CENTERS

People don't want to get rid of their televisions, but sometimes it's nice to hide TVs away for more family time and a cleaner aesthetic. Building a built-in bookshelf that spans your living room wall or an alcove with hidden doors above your fireplace has great appeal. Whether you have a large flatscreen that prioritizes the environment or a vintage television, you can build an entertainment center that tucks it out of sight whenever you want to unplug.

#8: JETTED BATHTUB

Going to the spa is always a treat, but you might not schedule appointments as often as you'd like. That's one reason homeowners are installing jetted bathtubs in their bathrooms. You can relax in luxury without leaving your home once you remodel your bathroom to fit your preferred jetted model. The simple element will help relieve your daily stress if you love to soak in a bubble bath.

#9: WALK-IN CLOSETS

Bigger closets give you more room to store your belongings, but they're so much more than storage space. They also add luxury to any home and create new opportunities for personalization. Consider remodeling your closet this year to include features like cabinets, built-in lighting, display shelves, and seating. You'll add value to your home and make it feel like a mansion. Plus, it's always helpful to have extra room for storing your belongings.

#10: KITCHEN REFRESH

When buyers are browsing real estate listings, many are seeking stunning kitchens with amazing details. If your home doesn't have this yet, upgrading the kitchen is one of the best renovations that you can do. That being said, kitchen remodels can be incredibly expensive. Still, you should also remember that the return on investment can be huge. Some sellers that renovated their kitchen before selling found that their home resale value rose by more than $80,000 after a kitchen remodel, and they even got multiple offers.

If comparable properties in your area have renovated kitchens, this will be a must if you want to increase your listing price. If properties do not have renovated kitchens, this might be a great time to stand out. To cut back on costs, consider only renovating part of the kitchen, especially if your kitchen is already partially updated.

You can spend less than $20,000 on renovations if you only update one or two of the following:
- Cabinetry
- Appliances
- Countertops
- Flooring
- Lighting and fixtures

Of course, consider your budget when choosing between these enhancements. It's OK if you cannot take on a huge renovation project. Even small investments can double back the money you earn at resale, so think logically as you plan your next steps.

ABOUT THE AUTHOR:

Merilee Kern, MBA is an internationally-regarded brand strategist and analyst who reports on noteworthy industry change makers, movers, shakers and innovators across all B2B and B2C categories. This includes field experts and thought leaders, brands, products, services, destinations and events. Merilee is Founder, Executive Editor and Producer of *"The Luxe List."* As a prolific business and consumer trends, lifestyle and leisure industry voice of authority and tastemaker, she keeps her finger on the pulse of the marketplace in search of new and innovative must-haves and exemplary experiences at all price points, from the affordable to the extreme—also delving into the minds behind the brands. Her work reaches multi-millions worldwide via broadcast TV (her own shows and copious others on which she appears) as well as a myriad of print and online publications. Some or all of the accommodations(s), experience(s), item(s) and/or service(s) detailed above may have been provided or arranged at no cost to accommodate if this is review editorial, but all opinions expressed are entirely those of Merilee Kern and have not been influenced in any way.

CONNECT WITH MERILEE

www.TheLuxeList.com
www.SavvyLiving.tv
www.Instagram.com/MerileeKern
www.Twitter.com/MerileeKern
www.Facebook.com/MerileeKernOfficial
www.LinkedIn.com/in/MerileeKern

The SHE RISES STUDIOS PODCAST

TUNE IN. RISE UP. THRIVE.

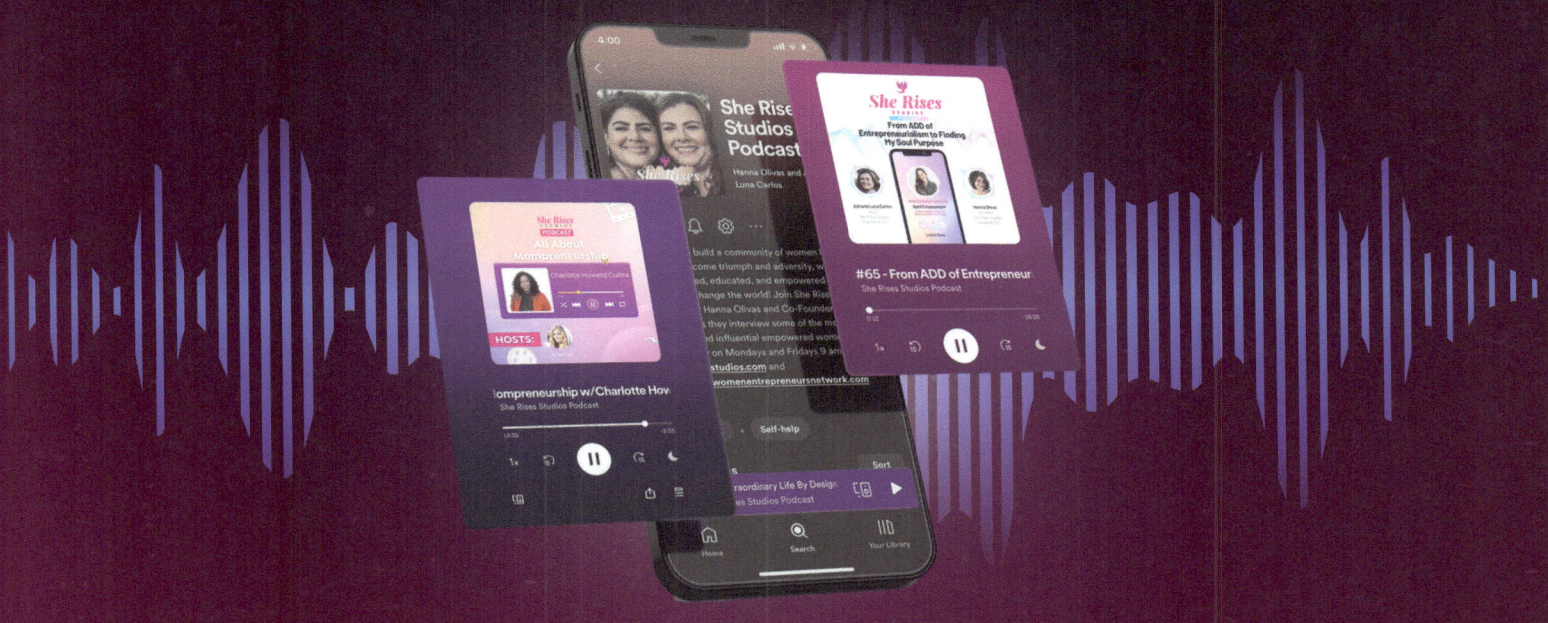

Looking for **real conversations** that inspire, empower, and ignite your potential? The **SRS Podcast** is where women like you come to **learn, grow, and rise!**

Join us for powerful **interviews with trailblazing entrepreneurs, thought leaders, and everyday women** who have turned obstacles into opportunities. Our episodes dive into:

➢ **Breaking through self-doubt** and stepping into confidence
➢ **Building a thriving business** with purpose and passion
➢ **Mastering work-life balance** without guilt
➢ **Leveling up your mindset, health, and career**
➢ **Finding your true purpose and living boldly**

Each episode is packed with **real stories, expert insights, and actionable strategies** to help you take your life to the next level. **This isn't just a podcast—it's your roadmap to success!**

SUBSCRIBE NOW AND START YOUR JOURNEY TO EMPOWERMENT!

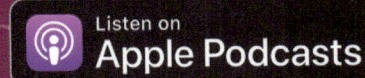

TIFFANY ALICHE:

THE BUDGETNISTA TRANSFORMING FINANCIAL FREEDOM FOR WOMEN

Tiffany Aliche, widely known as *"The Budgetnista,"* has become a leading force in financial education, empowering countless women to take control of their finances and build lasting wealth. Her journey from financial struggle to financial success has made her a relatable and inspiring figure in the personal finance space. Through her books, courses, and advocacy, Aliche has helped demystify money management, proving that financial freedom is attainable with the right tools and mindset.

Aliche's personal story is one of resilience and reinvention. After working as a preschool teacher for years, she found herself in a dire financial situation following the 2008 economic crisis. Facing job loss, mounting debt, and uncertainty, she immersed herself in learning the fundamentals of financial literacy. What she discovered transformed her own life, and she soon realized she could help others navigate their financial challenges as well. This led her to create The Budgetnista, a platform dedicated to educating individuals—particularly women—on budgeting, saving, and investing.

At the heart of Aliche's financial philosophy is the belief that knowledge is power. She has made it her mission to equip women with the education they need to make informed financial decisions. Her bestselling book, *Get Good with Money*, lays out a ten-step plan for achieving financial wholeness, covering everything from budgeting and debt repayment to retirement planning and estate management.

Unlike traditional financial advice that often feels overwhelming, Aliche's approach is straightforward, actionable, and designed to meet people where they are.

Beyond individual financial empowerment, Aliche has worked to enact systemic change. In 2019, she played a pivotal role in advocating for financial education legislation in New Jersey. As a result, the state passed a law requiring financial literacy instruction for middle school students, ensuring that younger generations develop essential money management skills early in life. This achievement underscores her belief that financial empowerment must be accessible to all, not just those who seek it out independently.

"THE MOST IMPORTANT ASPECT OF KEEPING YOUR MONEY IS BEING AWARE OF HOW MUCH OF IT YOU ARE SPENDING."

Aliche's impact aligns seamlessly with Success Savvy Magazine's April theme, *"Financial Futures: Empowering Path to Wealth and Success."* Her work demonstrates that financial independence is not just about income—it's about education, discipline, and strategic planning. By teaching women how to break free from financial insecurity and build sustainable wealth, she is shaping a future where financial stability is within reach for all. Through her unwavering commitment to financial literacy, Aliche is transforming lives, proving that true success begins with financial confidence and smart money management.

THE FIRST STEP TO FINANCIAL POWER?

ASK QUESTIONS, SAYS BELINDA SILVA

"I know what it's like to be in my clients' shoes," she says. *"Sometimes they need someone at the bank they can trust, and I strive to be that person."*

For many Latinos, money is a private topic, sometimes even an uncomfortable one, especially when it comes to asking for help. Belinda Silva wants to change that. As a consumer area manager at Bank of Oklahoma, she has spent years helping Latinos make informed financial decisions. But beyond offering guidance, she's working to change the mindset that keeps many from seeking financial resources in the first place: the fear of asking questions or admitting what they don't know.

Finding Purpose

Seven years ago, Silva moved from California to Tulsa with her husband and daughter to be closer to their family. What she found was a Latino community that shared a common hesitation toward banking. She made it her mission to change that.

But for Silva, financial empowerment isn't just about being a familiar face, it's about being active in the community. Therefore, she became more than just a banker, she strived to become a trusted voice.

Not only did she help develop Bank of Oklahoma's Hispanic/Latino strategy to expand financial access, but she also serves as a bridge in the community. She partners with organizations like UMA Tulsa and the Tulsa Latin American Chamber of Commerce, connecting Latino families and small business owners with financial education, business mentorship, and access to capital.

Silva understands that simply expanding access isn't enough; it's also important for people to feel comfortable reaching out for help in the first place.

The Power of Asking Questions

Many Latinos still hesitate to even step into a bank for fear of looking uninformed, therefore Silva works to shift that mindset, and actively encourages clients to rely on their bankers.

"Whenever there's a big financial decision, I tell my clients: go to your banker first," she says. *"If you're thinking about buying a house, go to your banker and start asking questions. If you're thinking about trading in your car, do the same. The first step should always be understanding your financial options—not walking into, say, a dealership or applying blindly for a loan."*

She wants Latinos to see banks as partners. Whether they need to understand loan qualifications, learn how to set up a savings plan, or look for funding for a business, she encourages them to be proactive about getting the information they need.

Taking Control

The financial system can feel overwhelming, but it isn't off-limits to those willing to ask the right questions. And while building a strong financial foundation takes time, it starts with a single step.

"People don't realize how much power they have over their financial future," Silva says. *"They just need to take the first step and get over their shame of not knowing all the answers. That's how everything starts."*

CONNECT WITH BELINDA

www.linkedin.com/in/belinda-silva-08015420a
www.bankofoklahoma.com

GET YOUR COPY NOW

Celebrate the power of women through inspiring stories and insights.

What the Funk?!
Molly Smith

Quantum Leaps and Lost Socks
Iman Kamel

Radiate: Unleash Your Inner Light
Raeyan Goff

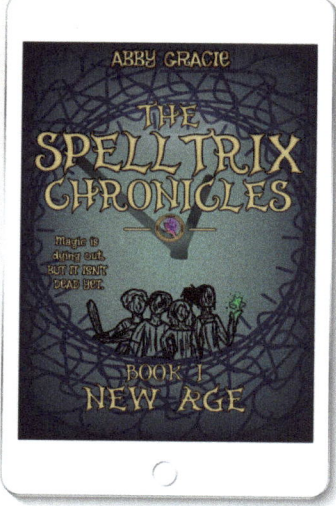

The Spelltrix Chronicles - Book 1 -
New Age - Abby Gracie

As if By Magic -
Lucy Kobier

SHE RISES
STUDIOS

*U*NLEASH YOUR STORY

BECOME A PUBLISHED AUTHOR!

Have you ever dreamed of sharing your wisdom, experience, or passion with the world? **Now is your time!**

Publishing a book isn't just about writing—it's about **establishing your authority, inspiring others, and creating a lasting legac**y. Plus, with the **$138.5 billion book industry** booming, there's never been a better moment to step into the spotlight.

At **SRS Publishing**, we don't just publish books—we **elevate voices, empower authors, and create change-makers**. Our mission is to help women break barriers, amplify their stories, and thrive in the publishing world. Whether you're an entrepreneur, thought leader, or storyteller at heart, **we're here to guide you every step of the way.**

JOIN THE FASTEST-GROWING PUBLISHING HOUSE FOR WOMEN IN THE USA.

READY TO TURN YOUR DREAM INTO REALITY?

 www.SheRisesStudios.com | *contact@sherisesstudios.com*